PRAISE FOR *CONSERVATIVE INSURGENCY*

"*Conservative Insurgency,* while a work of fiction, presents a plausible scenario for how conservative patriots can recapture the United States peacefully, and from within. Like its author, my friend Kurt Schlichter, it is passionately optimistic about America and Americans, and about the eventual triumph of liberty. But Kurt's optimism isn't rooted in his disposition alone. He truly believes in the manifest superiority of the American idea and, ultimately, in the determination, grit and perseverance of his fellow believers to restore it. This book does way more than entertain; it informs, it instructs, it motivates, and it energizes us. Unlike far too many conservatives, Army colonel-trial lawyer-political commentator-stand-up-comic Kurt Schlichter refuses to surrender the nation he loves. In this book he shares with us, from a future perspective, how many likeminded Americans rejected defeat and saved America from the ravages of progressivism and for our posterity. A fascinating read."

—DAVID LIMBAUGH,
Bestselling author and conservative commentator

"Since 2012, a lot of folks on the Right have shared an ominous mood that for most Americans, life will get worse before it gets better. Kurt Schlichter offers a pugnacious, funny, no-holds-barred, wild, epic political adventure story that assures us that delays are not denials and that the appeal of liberty never dies.

Kurt uses wit and sarcasm the way a samurai wields his long and short swords. "The Conservative Insurgency is a sharp and incisive battle plan in novel form, a legendary tale to stir the heart of every happy warrior..

Kurt's ffuture scenario envisions 'members of the insurgency gravitating to media and entertainment organically'—a process that perhaps this novel will accelerate."

–JIM GERAGHTY,
National Review columnist and bestselling author

"Here's how the conservative movement won—from 30 years in the future. Kurt Schlichter's creative and fascinating take on how conservatives can achieve victory is an optimistic breath of fresh air in a dark time."

—BEN SHAPIRO,
Bestselling author, conservative columnist and radio host

"Please, God, make it so. Not the part about Bobby Jindal only getting to be VP, but at least 90% of Kurt's crystal ball look into what could be, not what has been; how things could turn, not as they are likely to turn out right now. Schlichter's genius—and it is genius—is to make it all possible based upon a single premise: That conservatives will play to win. A stretch of course, an enormous stretch, but not greater than that of 1776, 1789, 1860, 1944 or 1980. Read it and be inspired."

—HUGH HEWITT,
Bestselling author, commentator and national radio host

Conservative Insurgency does not just paint a picture of how conservatives can take back the country, it does so using a concept few conservatives use—an actual story as opposed to a rote polemical tirade. This is a great read, provides a good way forward, and offers a new concept for how conservatives should be writing books about their future.

—ERICK ERICKSON,
Fox News Commentator,
Redstate.com editor and radio host

"This book is exactly the electric jolt of inspiration that grassroots activists on the Right need. Conservative Insurgency imagines what American life would be like in 2041 if constitutional principles of limited government prevailed: healthier, wealthier, happier, and free. But it's more than a vision. It's a call to arms. Herein lies a strategic battle plan for bold action against progressive enslavement on all fronts—political, social, and cultural. Thank you, Colonel Schlichter. I'm energized and ready to fight!"

— MICHELLE MALKIN,
Bestselling author and Fox News commentator

"What Kurt Schlichter has given us with *Conservative Insurgency* is hope for a future that seems too good to be true. This is his *Gone with the Wind*, but in a world where *Gone with the Wind* isn't an oppressively awful book that people only read when forced to by a professor who needs to free up time for 'office hours' with a hot grad student.

Schlichter gives us that world. He also serves notice to the dominant and often indistinguishable major political parties in the United States that if the Republic survives, they will not in their present forms. *Conservative Insurgency* paints a future America that's being run by Americans who like being Americans, which is a radical notion indeed."

—STEPHEN KRUISER,
Conservative comic, commentator and author

"*Conservative Insurgency* captures the spirit of my friend Andrew Breitbart with a no-holds-barred, bare-knuckle brawl for the heart and soul of our country."

—DANA LOESCH,
BlazeTV host and Fox News commentator

"This isn't your father's political affairs book. A perfect rebuttal for those who say conservatism is stuck in the past. By turns sobering and delightfully devilish, Kurt Schlichter takes no prisoners in telling the story of how a small group of Americans turned their country around."

—CAM EDWARDS,
Host of Cam and Company on Sirius XM Radio,
The Sportsman Channel and NRA News

"Simultaneously a grim look at our country's near future and an exhilarating blueprint for America's survival in the long haul, Kurt Schlichter's *Conservative Insurgency* will make you laugh, grit your teeth, nod your head, and gird your loins for the long battle against the progressives that all freedom-loving Americans face over the next two or three generations. Extrapolating horrendous liberal policies to their inexorable conclusions, and with a pitch-perfect understanding of the hearts and minds of both progressives and conservatives, Schlichter grimly lays the horrors of the coming years all out for us, and consoles us with laughter, truth, hope, and the prescription for the remedies—as well as a much-needed swift kick in the ass."

—NICK SEARCY,
International Stage and Screen Actor

"Excellent! It turns out we are the ones we've been waiting for, and they're not. Kurt Schlichter wonderfully imagines a future we can only pray for, a future in which those who believe in liberty and the Constitution rise up as one and take America back from the Obamas and the Hillarys and the whole ceaselessly destructive hive-mind of the left. It actually can happen here—and we better damn well hope it does."

—ANDREW KLAVAN,
Bestselling author and conservative commentator

"Kurt Schlichter will have heads exploding at Media Matters, MSNBC and the rest of the progressive world (or imploding since vacuums collapse on themselves), but patriots will be laughing and cheering. *Conservative Insurgency* is as much a roadmap as it is a cautionary tale. He sees where the country is going and lays out how to correct it. I just hope his words are taken to heart and we don't have to wait until 2041 for it to happen. The iceberg didn't swerve and the Titanic lost. We are on a path toward our own iceberg, but we still have some time, and Kurt has shown us the way."

—DEREK HUNTER,
Conservative columnist and radio host

CONSERVATIVE INSURGENCY

THE STRUGGLE TO TAKE AMERICA BACK: 2009–2041

KURT SCHLICHTER

A POST HILL PRESS BOOK

CONSERVATIVE INSURGENCY
The Struggle to Take America Back: 2009–2041
© 2014 Kurt Schlichter

ISBN (hardcover): 978-1-61868-977-1
ISBN (eBook): 978-1-61868-978-8

Published by Post Hill Press
109 International Drive, Suite 300
Franklin, TN 37067

Cover design by Sean Salter
Supplemental design by Travis Franklin
Interior book design by Neuwirth & Associates, Inc.

Visit us online at http://posthillpress.com

ACKNOWLEDGMENTS

It is only fair to share the credit, or the blame, for this book. There are many folks who provided assistance of many kinds. I'll try to name as many as I can, but please forgive the oversight if I miss someone, which I undoubtedly will.

First, there is my hot wife, Irina Moises. She put up with this latest insanity, like all the other insanities that came before.

Mom and Dad, thanks!

Thanks to my agent, Jennifer Cohen, who shepherded this through the process. Thanks also to the Post Hill Press team, especially, Anthony Ziccardi. Along the way, David Limbaugh and Adam Bellow provided a lot of good advice.

I got plenty of support from my friends Larry O'Connor, Cam Edwards, Cameron Gray, Tony Katz, Ben Shapiro, Hugh Hewitt, Erick Erickson, Dana and Chris Loesch, Jim Geraghty, Nick Searcy, Michelle Malkin, Adam Baldwin, Greg Garrison, and Derek Hunter. Drew and Sue Matich, Stephen Kruiser, Owen Brennan, Larry Correia, Andrew Klavan, and Michael Walsh also provided some great suggestions. And I took a lot of ideas from the writings aggregated at Glenn Reynolds's

Instapundit site, which has been my first read of the day for over a dozen years.

I wish Andrew Breitbart were still around to thank. I expect he is looking down, smiling.

And there are more—Kellie Jane Adan, Kim Tabin Mann, Kevin McKeever, Sean "Salty Hollywood" Salter, Gary and Shelli Eaton, Fingers Malloy, Thomas LaDuke, Bruce Carroll, Jimmie Bise, Jr., Daniel Deaton (CAPT, USN, retired), and many others who I have met within the real-life conservative insurgency.

And, of course, I want to thank all of my Twitter followers for all of their caring!

CONTENTS

A NOTE ON DEFINITIONS AND USAGE

Throughout this book, the interview subjects (and the author) refer to the two main political forces in conflict in American politics between 2009 and 2041 by a variety of terms. This leads to occasional imprecision, since the terms are not necessarily synonymous.

For example, those on the right can generally be referred to as "conservatives," but the activist, small government conservatives who made up the conservative insurgency discussed here seem to prefer the more precise term of "constitutional conservatives." This distinguishes them from what they would call "establishment conservatives," who they would often deny were conservatives at all.

There is considerable overlap between the "constitutional conservatives" and the "Tea Party," though the term Tea Party lost favor in the 2010s and was rarely used after 2016 except by its opponents. They used it as an epithet, sometimes very effectively.

The term "Republicans" is ambiguous because there was often open conflict within the Republican Party between the old-guard establishment and the constitutional conservatives.

The constitutional conservatives would often label moderate Republicans RINOs (Republicans In Name Only), though that species became less and less common as the party moved right throughout the 2010s and 2020s.

When describing their opponents on the left side of the spectrum, the constitutional conservatives tended to use various terms nearly interchangeably: progressive, liberal, and even leftist. This can be confusing because progressives, liberals, and leftists see themselves as quite different even if no one else tends to. Moreover, there were "progressive Republicans," exemplified by Senator John McCain, who shared a faith in government action, if little else, with leftist progressives.

The Democratic Party became much more ideologically homogenous earlier than the GOP; by the mid-2000s, when Senator Joe Lieberman was effectively expelled, there were no arguably "conservative" major Democratic figures. Accordingly, "Democrat" became synonymous with "liberal" in conservative circles, even if Democrats themselves would rarely use the terms that way.

Imputing too much precision into these imprecise terms is an invitation to confusion, and there seems little benefit in the form of a greater understanding to be had from undertaking that burden. In order to avoid attempting to divine each speaker's intent as to his usage of the various terms, they are simply transcribed verbatim. The reader may evaluate them for himself in the context in which they appear.

CONSERVATIVE
INSURGENCY

INTRODUCTION

I originally raised the idea of writing an oral history of the conservative movement that arose during the first Barack Obama administration with the head of the University of California, San Diego, History Department two years ago. I was a bit surprised by his reaction—instead of encouraging me, he attempted to talk me out of it.

Jeff Rayburn was a West Pointer and a decorated war hero of Afghanistan and Iraq whose hard-core conservative views mirrored those of better than half the faculty in the new academia of the mid-twenty-first century. One might think that he would be excited about one of his department members undertaking a project that would track how a disorganized, decentralized band of committed citizens he supported had managed to create not only political but cultural change that sent the

United States on an entirely new sociopolitical trajectory in just 30 years.

"Do we really need another book on how wonderful conservatives are?" he asked me, sounding bored. "I've got a shelf full of them. Hell, I *wrote* one."

It was true, literally. In Jeff's office there is a bookcase full of hardcovers dealing with modern conservative politics—to this day he refuses to read books on electronic devices—and one of them, a bestseller in fact, he wrote.

But I was looking to do something else. My goal is not to praise the movement but to let it speak for itself. What interested me—and what I hope the stories I have collected here cast some light on—is how a discredited, dispirited, and government-targeted ideology morphed into a movement that overcame the liberal establishment.

"You know what you're talking about," Jeff said off-handedly, "is an insurgency. I know one when I see one because I fought a couple of them. It was a conservative insurgency that changed America. A small, dedicated group, defying a corrupt, decrepit authority, and winning through persistence and dedication."

That idea formed the nucleus of this book, a book about how regular Americans not only seized control of the apparatus of government but won over society itself to its worldview.

■ ■ ■

As a historian, documenting the conservative insurgency was a challenge because of its very nature. This was not the story of a single "great man" who came along at just the moment his country needed him. There is no Washington, Lincoln, King, or even a Reagan whose biography I could use as a means to tell the story of the struggle. While many of the individuals who rose to prominence during this process were notable for their foresight, courage, and wisdom, in retrospect these leaders were largely fungible. No one name comes to mind when we think about the last 30 years.

This was not a top-down movement but one created, motivated, and executed from the bottom up. Franklin Roosevelt will be forever linked with the New Deal, and Ronald Reagan with the "Reagan Revolution," but there was no single man or woman who led this revolution. Instead, it was thousands, and then millions, of individuals whose decentralized actions changed the course of American history.

I can best tell their collective story by letting them each tell their own individual stories in their own words.

Although more than 300 million Americans lived through the tumultuous events of the last three decades, we do not all share the same perspective on them. For instance, as a young academic at the time, I was largely unaware of just how great the impact of the Obama administration's policies was upon a huge swath of American citizens. I heard President Obama promise to "fundamentally transform" the nature of our country, and I nodded at what I saw as a pleasing rhetorical flourish and went about my life, as did many similarly situated, moderately liberal Americans. But conservative Americans heard this and were chilled to the bone. Their worst fears were proven true as the Obama administration moved relentlessly to impose its liberal vision upon them and what they saw as the country they had built with their sweat and blood.

Obama came to office in the wake of a sudden, paradigm-rattling economic crisis caused not by the usual ups and downs associated with the business cycle but by large, government-connected businesses whose reckless actions brought the country to the brink of catastrophe. The response to this crisis, declared a bipartisan establishment within a matter of days after its leaders emerged from closed-door consultations, was to be a giant government bailout.

Of course, the great American middle class had long been "bailing out" the poor with social programs. It perceived these transfers of wealth as at least marginally justifiable, though it generally conceived them as going to ameliorate self-induced social pathologies.

The middle class had likewise been bailing out the wealthy elite—"corporate welfare" had long been a fixture of the liberal critique of the system—but the beneficiaries had heretofore wisely kept that web of subsidies, tax breaks, and special privileges largely out of sight. However, there was no hiding the TARP bailout, nor the fact that it was imposed without meaningful debate via the consensus of the elite over the objections of Middle America.

Middle America saw itself pushed to the sidelines by a coalition of the very poor and the very powerful. It was expected to wait silently as the nation's fate was decided by others, while it was also expected to continue to work hard and to pick up the tab.

The Tea Party revolt of the first Obama term was a direct reaction to Middle America being excluded from power. The Tea Party movement was fueled by a critique of the establishment that centered on the primacy of the Constitution as written and a suspicion of the poor/powerful coalition of government rent seekers. What distinguished it was its bottom-up nature—it was organized not by a formal cadre of "community organizers" (the left's preferred model) but by individuals spontaneously springing into action across the country. Traditionally entrepreneurial—it is no surprise that many Tea Party activists were small business people and that their targets included the large corporations that succeeded largely through government lobbying—these activists turned those skills from commerce to politics. Soon, seemingly overnight, hundreds of Tea Party–affiliated groups were up and operating.

The establishment took notice and, in conjunction with a mainstream media that absolutely toed the establishment line, reacted. It was not merely the Democrats who did so. Moderate Republicans whose view of big government could be summed up as, "Well, okay, we'll expand it, but not quite so much right now," were especially threatened. They were as much a part of the status quo as any overt Democrat statist. So, before the Tea Party could take on the Democrats and return America to what it saw as its traditional politics, the insurgents needed to seize control of the GOP. That meant that the first targets for the Tea Party were other "conservatives" who were not quite so conservative in practice.

In 2010, Tea Party activism—supercharged by the Democrats' ram-through of the disastrous Obamacare medical insurance reform plan—led to the recapture of the House of Representatives. But it was much less successful in 2012, when several Tea Party–associated candidates made rookie mistakes that likely cost the GOP the Senate—although it was less widely noted at the time that several "traditional" Republican candidates also lost what should have been easy races even as Obama was reelected.

Over the years following Obama's reelection, the Tea Party fought on two fronts, both against a liberal administration that was attempting to translate a slim electoral victory into a mandate to move even harder left and a GOP establishment that was reluctant to fight for the principles it paid lip service to during the campaign. The conservatives, labeled the "Tea Party" even though that name had less and less meaning over time, forced

5

a confrontation with the administration that led to a short government shutdown. GOP moderates engineered a capitulation, hoping this defeat for their internal opponents would quell the rebellion forever.

The anti-Tea Party reaction was vicious, and its excesses went hand-in-hand with the other actions of the Obama administration that demonstrated to the budding insurgents that America was being fundamentally changed for the worst. The media and popular culture savaged the Tea Party, painting it as racist, as crypto-fascist, and astonishingly, as a tool of the very large corporations the Tea Party itself opposed. Vilified in polite society, the Tea Party—or, rather, the label "Tea Party"—largely vanished. But the insurgency it had sparked only grew.

That growth was fueled by the plummeting credibility and the increasing lawlessness of the Obama administration. Within weeks of the ignominious end of the shutdown, the fiasco that was Obamacare became undeniable. The website that allowed users to participate in the insurance exchanges simply failed to function. While this embarrassing lapse would be remedied over time, the fact that the law would throw millions of Americans off their insurance plans in favor of new, Obamacare-friendly plans that covered needs they didn't have with higher deductibles at much higher prices could not.

While moderates hesitated, grassroots conservatives savaged the administration for its outright lies, producing video compilations of Obama promising Americans, "If you like your plan, you can keep it." The liberal media was forced to take the position that millions of infuriated Americans should have known better than to believe what they were told. It was a harsh, but indelible, lesson for millions of Americans who had bought into the idea of "hope and change."

Frustrated by an opposition that dared to defy it, as time wore on the Obama administration and its liberal allies would reject the norms that had previously governed American politics and act without regard to the customs, practices, and even laws that had restrained previous presidents. It turned the Internal Revenue Service on Tea Party–aligned groups. It ended the 200-year-old tradition of the filibuster in the Senate. As the curtain came down on the Obama presidency, the liberal establishment began to actively seek to suppress free speech. Power prevailed over principle, and the conflict within the culture intensified.

This trend would continue through the Hillary Clinton administration. It would eventually lead to liberalism's defeat as ascendant conservatives mercilessly dismantled the welfare state while liberals watched helplessly, their power to stop it hamstrung by the very majoritarian precedents they had used to build it.

The Obama administration and the liberal establishment's exercise of raw power began early. They passed a huge stimulus in the first months of 2009 without any bipartisan support. It was, essentially, a trillion dollar payoff to Democratic voting blocs. It did nothing for the economy, which would languish throughout both the Obama and Clinton administrations. They forced through the failed Obamacare plan without a single Republican vote, choosing to reorganize a sixth of the economy over the objections of every single member of the opposition. Obamacare's utter failure, which could not be foisted off on liberalism's opponents, would be one of the weights that would help drag liberalism down.

The Obama administration's lawlessness, and Clinton's choice to follow her predecessor's path, not only sparked anger and distrust in government that fed the insurgency but made compromise impossible. By turning the Internal Revenue Service and other agencies on its political enemies (whether Obama himself knew about the targeting, or whether he merely created an atmosphere that tolerated such un-American activities, remains unclear even now), the Obama administration undercut the moral legitimacy of the federal government. By refusing to enforce laws it disapproved of, such as the crucial enforcement provisions of the carefully crafted comprehensive immigration reform legislation pushed through with the help of the GOP establishment, the Obama administration made compromise impossible. It simply could not be trusted to perform its part of any bargain, so there would be no further bargains.

The standoff in Washington begun after the Tea Party–fueled takeover of the House in 2010 continued after the brutal 2014 midterm election season. The passage of the comprehensive immigration reform law—an inexplicable lifeline tossed to Obama at his nadir by big business interests and Republican moderates—split the GOP, and the Republicans' dream of retaking the Senate floundered. Even with Obamacare failing before the electorate's eyes, the GOP barely held the House.

The Obama administration doubled-down on its embrace of executive power, largely ignoring the Congress and seizing new powers through the administrative state during its last two years. These abuses of power continued, and the Clinton administration likewise made little effort to hide its use of government agencies to punish its enemies and reward its friends.

Yet the conservative insurgency grew with each new overreach and each new abuse. The seeds the Tea Party had planted a few years before were sprouting. Activists who had been inspired to take seats on school boards, local Republican committees, and the like now had several years of experience governing as well as enthusiasm. Out in the hinterlands, under the media's radar and operating where grassroots power could have the greatest effect, they began to have an impact. A growing farm team of conservative leaders was developing, gaining experience, and waiting to move up the ladder.

Insurgents fought back against liberal power grabs in court, recognizing that because the largely liberal judiciary would ignore the law, the real value of the judicial process in the short term was as political theater to highlight liberal wrongdoing. The courts themselves aided the cause by overstepping. Hillary Clinton's replacement for Anthony Kennedy, a liberal feminist academic like most of her appointees, tipped the balance of the Supreme Court hard to the left and drove millions of formerly passive Americans into the insurgency. She was placed on the Court only because the Democrats eliminated the last vestige of the traditional filibuster, a maneuver they would come to regret.

In 2018, the Supreme Court had issued rulings to the effect that the Second Amendment did not mean what it expressly said, but that the Constitution's silence on the issue of abortion somehow indicated the Founders' clear intent that the government would pay for them. Moreover, the justices found a provision lurking within the Constitution holding that doctors could be ordered to perform abortions regardless of their religious objections. Such decisions inspired a campaign of civil—and not so civil—disobedience that in turn called down harsher repression from the Clinton regime. It was a classic insurgency phenomenon—a government further undercutting its own legitimacy by overreaction to the insurgents, who then capitalized on the overreaction to amplify the cycle once again.

The surveillance state the Obama administration oversaw drove young people away from the smothering embrace of liberalism, though not immediately into the insurgency. It was only as the insurgency demonstrated that "social issues" were not its focus, contrary to the portrayals of an increasingly hysterical mainstream media, that young people began to consider the "liberty option" that the insurgency offered. The fact that liberal economic policies had led to 45 percent unemployment among debt-ridden recent college graduates in 2019 made the conservative alternative that much more appealing.

The Obama administration had fitfully started reexamining long-term issues like drug and federal criminal law reform, but it had predictably done so not through legislation but with uncoordinated and poorly thought-through executive actions. Hillary Clinton, whose authoritarian instincts at home came to define her presidency as much as her inept foreign policy abroad, quickly undid even these minor changes. With the crime rate growing, she sought to get to the conservatives' right on the issue. The insurgency's willingness to let her do so, and to consider more humane and wise drug law and sentencing reforms, provided a key opening into the once solid-Democrat minority voting bloc.

Clinton's contempt for individual rights, and a Supreme Court willing to limit free speech rights where they threatened the establishment's hold on power, drove even more formerly apolitical Americans into the arms of the conservative insurgency. Many former liberals joined the insurgency too, often contending (not unlike Ronald Reagan did with regard to the Democratic Party) that they had not left liberalism but that liberalism had left them. But it also set up a challenge for the insurgency that it continues to face today—would the nontraditional strategies and tactics it felt compelled to adopt to compete with the liberal establishment make reinstating a traditional America impossible?

America found itself on the brink of the abyss during the second Clinton term. Abroad, the military was a hollow shell and the United States was regularly humiliated by foreign potentates who had nothing but contempt for Clinton's weakness. A botched invasion of the Iranian coast in response to its terrible nuclear strike on Israel on November 30, 2020, led to years of humiliation over the prisoners of war abandoned after Clinton's panicked retreat order.

At home, the economy was moribund, with the "new normal" being a lack of upward mobility for the declining cohort of Americans who still sought to work rather than to collect government checks. Worse, as the insurgency grew, the liberal establishment's desperate grip on power tightened. The administration harassed, abused, and sometimes even arrested its opponents. It clumsily attempted to suppress dissent, whether on the Internet or in the media. And there was violence, as administration-affiliated thugs intimidated designated "enemies" and as states acted to nullify unconstitutional laws. The shootout at an Austin, Texas, airfield between federal marshals trying to enforce Clinton's federal handgun ban and Texas Rangers determined to stop them left several dead. It could have easily been the first battle in a very different insurgency, one that involved violence instead of peaceful political action.

By the end of the Clinton administration, Americans had a choice. And thanks to the conservative insurgency, there was a viable alternative to both the intellectually and politically exhausted liberalism of Obama and Clinton and to the status quo–embracing moderate Republicanism of the John McCains of the GOP. Conservative think tanks had a ready supply of policy prescriptions for the problems facing the country. The mainstream media, thanks to technological changes that bypassed liberal gatekeeping and to infiltration by committed conservatives, was no longer the pro-establishment monolith of the past. Out in the states, conservatives had taken power and demonstrated that the vision of the insurgents would work in practice.

But, most of all, there was now a generation of insurgents ready to take power—and the last 16 years of defying the liberal establishment's merciless counterinsurgency had endowed them with a ruthlessness that would ensure they would not hesitate to aggressively impose their conservative vision when given the chance. That ethic remains today within the conservative movement, even as critics now question whether the movement has strayed too far from the norms and values it had sought to revitalize.

But such considerations paled in comparison with the need for expediency in seizing back the apparatus of the federal government. The insurgency's chance came in 2024, when the governor of Florida was elected president over yet another doctrinaire liberal. President Carrie Marlowe was less significant as an individual than as a representative of the insurgency.

Liberalism's aging playbook simply did not apply when faced with what she represented. It was hard to decry a "War on Women" when, like perhaps a majority of insurgency activists, Marlowe was a woman. Other conservative women had been targeted in the past, but Marlowe cleverly sidestepped such political land mines as abortion by refusing to take a national position and insisting—in keeping with the firm federalist inclinations of the insurgency—that the issue be remanded to the states. That, in conjunction with a cultural turn against the idea of abortion, brought the Bill Clinton formulation of abortion as "safe, legal, and rare" to fruition. Today, only eight states allow it, and combined with society's distaste for it, the numbers are a fraction of those in the past. However, the Marlowe compromise did not completely disarm the issue—it still comes up in Republican primaries today, with no sign of it ever being completely resolved on the horizon.

Marlowe also set out to redefine the GOP's relationship with minorities. Her sentencing reform platform and active outreach to minorities, which she began as Florida's governor, earned her a hearing with minority voters not offered to other Republicans. While she did not win a majority of minority votes, she won more than the Democrats could afford to lose.

As would be expected from one of the insurgents, she refused to apologize for America—she radiated pride in the nation while promising to reign in the excesses of the oppressive surveillance state. Her steely ultimatum to the Iranians following her inauguration solved the prisoner crisis in hours, echoing Ronald Reagan's resolution of the hostage crisis 44 years before.

After nearly two decades of ennui, Americans were ready not only to have pride again, but to have a nation worthy of pride again.

Of course, the political result was only one consequence of the conservative insurgency's cultural campaign. After all, "politics," as the late Andrew Breitbart famously observed, "is downstream from culture." The insurgency was never about just winning political offices. Rather, constitutional conservatives winning political offices in large numbers came only *after* constitutional conservatives began winning the cultural struggle.

On the macro side, the insurgency targeted media and entertainment—or, more accurately, members of the insurgency gravitated to media and entertainment organically. Developments in technology meant that participation in media and entertainment was no longer restricted to large, well-funded corporations. Even individuals could create media products and, just as importantly, distribute them to consumers.

Moreover, conservatives themselves stopped self-selecting against careers in the media and entertainment industries. They now went into those fields, expecting to compete even in the face of prejudice by the entrenched elite. As it became obvious that the sexism and racism attributed to conservatives was mere slander, the artificial social barriers to entry into the cultural industries fell. Conservatives began to be seen as regular people again. No longer could they be dismissed as sexist, racist, or homophobic and thereby be marginalized and ignored.

At the same time, these industries were facing more competition for customers and could no longer afford to contemptuously ignore the huge potential market that expressly conservative Americans represented. In the Obama years, Hollywood tentatively explored appealing to these customers, starting with reality shows. When a television program about a real-life family of bearded, backwoods, explicitly Christian hunters called *Duck Dynasty* set viewing records in the early 2010s, the industry took notice.

Soon, even the traditional networks were running shows where the explicitly conservative characters were the heroes and liberals were the butts of the jokes. In music, books, theater, and art, artists took tentative steps to reappraise traditional values and even embrace them. Americans, faced with their own experience of liberal failure, were receptive. But there was a brutal cultural backlash—old outlets like the *New York Times* savaged any dissent from liberal dogma when it could not ignore it. Yet the market for dissent was there, and as the failure of liberalism became more self-evident, one could see the late-night comics aiming their wit at Obama and Clinton with ever-increasing intensity. The cultural consensus, inspired in large part by liberalism's manifest failure, slowly changed to first accept conservatism, then embrace it. The insurgents locked in their victories. Marlowe—aided by the strong majorities in Congress that had come from the insurgent ground game (an organizational campaign facilitated by the technological mastery of many new adherents)—acted with an aggressiveness that stunned the liberal establishment. Obamacare had alienated millions of Americans with both its substantive failure and the government's shameful abuse of the private medical information it held to embarrass the administration's foes. Though many establishment Republicans had given up on ever repealing Obamacare, signing its repeal was one of Marlowe's first acts.

And she replaced it with . . . nothing. Conservatives felt that the federal government had no business in the health care field, and they acted on that principle. They offered no "alternative." The insurgents upended the paradigm by refusing to remain within the envelope the establishment had defined.

Firmly in control of the federal government, the constitutional conservatives repealed a mass of other additional health care statutes and regulations as well, and left it to individuals (and individual states, if they chose) to take responsibility for their health care in a free market. The market responded with a tsunami of new options. Some people without health insurance chose to be without it, instead wanting to pay cash, while others unwisely risked the consequences of forgoing coverage knowing that they were on their own.

Next, Marlowe and her Congress proceeded to gut the rest of the welfare state, slashing those programs they did not entirely eliminate. They bombed the rubble of the liberal establishment.

This return to personal responsibility culminated in the ratification of the Thirty-Second Amendment, which placed the responsibility for each individual's self-support unequivocally upon the individual himself. The insurgents (who still felt themselves fighting a lonely battle against the establishment even though they now held the reins of power) were not content to just prune the branches of the tree but instead, as one exasperated liberal senator put it, "dig out the roots and sow the ground with salt." The size of government at the end of Marlowe's second term, in *actual* dollars, was just over half the size of when she took office—and that took into account her massive rebuilding of America's shamefully degraded military.

The Obama and Clinton administrations had taught the insurgents a lesson that more traditional conservatives found difficult to accept—a disregard for old norms and traditions that would restrain their actions. They had attempted to evade GOP power in the Congress through executive orders; now, Marlowe used the same executive power remorselessly to dismantle the bureaucracy and impose her will. Liberals, frustrated by filibusters that obstructed their initiatives, had repealed the ancient senatorial rule years before; insurgents now gleefully passed dozens of bills that gutted liberal programs while liberals watched helplessly. Their passionate speeches full of renewed fear of majoritarian rule were met with howls of laughter.

They had handed the conservatives the sword that slew the liberal welfare state.

But the raw exercise of unconstrained power in a democratic republic is hardly conservative. The insurgency's stated goal was always to return to the Founders' ideal, but the realities of the battle it faced required putting off that restoration. Even today, the norms and customs that preceded the Obama administration have not been completely restored. A generation of conservatives has arisen that never experienced them; they largely know only political/cultural warfare in which principle does not always take priority over expedience.

Marlowe's "conservative court packing" illustrated the challenge. Faced with a liberal Supreme Court, Marlowe did not hesitate—not even for a second—to drive the impeachment of three liberal justices so she could pack the Court with insurgent jurists. She did the same in lesser courts—Obama had overseen the end of the filibuster to create a majority on the Court of Appeals for the District of Columbia Circuit, and Marlowe engineered a scheme to repack it by adding 10 new seats.

These, and other similarly aggressive actions, brought howls of outrage from liberals. A few more traditional conservative voices objected, but in vain. Sixteen years of facing ruthless aggression by the Obama and Clinton administrations had left the insurgents utterly indifferent to their objections and pleas for mercy.

Liberals made politics a zero-sum blood sport but forgot that the rules would apply to their opponents when they got the ball. It remains to be seen how well the insurgents have learned the same lesson.

Today, America defines itself as a "conservative" nation, but it is a different conservatism than the one that existed in 2008. Gone are many of the issues that fueled the national debate back then. Gay Americans are accepted with little or no thought to their orientation. Abortion, though still occasionally bubbling up to cause rifts between conservatives, was essentially papered over by being punted to the states. Marijuana is legal (though scorned by most American as hopelessly tacky), while laws regarding more serious drugs are much less severe. Women operate at the highest levels of the GOP without comment; in fact, women were at the forefront of the insurgency. The ubiquitous charges of racism hurled by liberals lack potency where a slim majority of Americans (including conservatives) classify themselves as "multiracial."

These changes came less as a result of ideological shifts on the part of conservatism but as a result of the necessary ideological winnowing process the conservative insurgency underwent as it built and grew and fought. Conservatives were forced to make choices, both about where to focus their efforts and about which issues would harm the cause and which would help it. Some issues, hugely important in 2009, are essentially meaningless today in 2041.

The insurgency succeeded by not creating a rigid checklist of many specific, and mandatory, policy prescriptions. The liberals had built up their own inflexible, immutable list, and they were bound to it. Their positions were based less on principles than on the needs and demands of each of the Democratic Party's myriad interest groups. Unions had their demands, for example, and those demands were incorporated into the checklist regardless of whether they supported or undercut some overarching principle. It created intellectual incoherence and a huge vulnerability to a principled opponent. When Carrie Marlowe and the GOP took back power in 2024, they were able to do so in part because the Democrats were so inflexible in their positions that the insurgents were able to outmaneuver them again and again. The liberals locked themselves into a platform of failure.

The insurgents, on the other hand, were able to succeed because they embraced a few general principles. They wanted a small government of limited powers, a federal government that stayed out of people's lives and focused on the relatively few tasks given it under the Constitution, like national defense.

They wanted a culture where self-reliance was assumed, and where powerful elites did not control and plunder the country without restraint. They wanted their rights honored, including the right to speak freely, to practice their religion, and to keep and bear arms. Importantly, for the surveillance state revelations drove many libertarians to the insurgency, they demanded that the government respect the privacy of its citizens.

The insurgents, in sum, rejected the liberal establishment's authoritarian, poor/powerful coalition's dominance. However, their response to that dominant liberal paradigm disregarded many of the same political and cultural norms and customs they sought to restore. That tension between principle and expedience remains today. The insurgency is ascendant; regardless of how it sees itself, it is no longer the *insurgency* but the *establishment*.

But the question remains—made even more pressing by the recent GOP corruption scandals—whether principle or expedience will prevail. Governance is far different than insurgency.

Even as it faces the challenges of the present, the conservative movement can look back on a remarkable achievement. The story of the insurgency is not the story of a great leader. Rather, it is the story of a great *people*, a people who refused to allow their nation to be taken from them while being handed the bill. Taking as inspiration the wise authors of a document that was two-and-a-half centuries old, and acting largely as individuals in the face of the scorn and sometimes even active oppression by the establishment, they took their country back.

This is their story.

PROLOGUE

"I still don't understand it," she sighs, staring out the plate-glass window overlooking San Francisco Bay. "In 2009, we were on the verge of truly transforming this country. We progressives had won the argument. We had the conservatives beat. And now . . . I just don't understand." She looks at me dead on, her wet eyes equal parts baffled and furious.

"*How* did this happen?"

It's overcast and cold outside, the mid-January gloom mirroring Gail Partridge's mood. At 64, she is still the "Proud Voice of Progressivism" and currently the star host on the Quantum satellite/web radio network. Her commitment to the liberal cause is literally a part of her. Poking out beneath the left sleeve of her floral blouse, etched into her wrinkled bicep, is the lower half of a tattoo of a face. If you concentrate, you can make out the mouth and jaw of Barack Obama. His visage has aged with her.

"They made progressivism a joke," she mutters. "Bastards."

In three days, the third conservative president in a row will be inaugurated. As what today we know as "constitutional conservatives" lock in their political power—and more importantly, their grip on American culture—it seemed appropriate to spend time with a legendary *bête noire* of the right.

When I messaged her requesting an interview, she was suspicious. "Are you some sort of right-wing hack writing another book about the glories of being heartless?" she had asked. "Are you one of *them*?"

That was a very good question, and it goes to the heart of this story.

I told her the truth, which is that I am a professor of history and politics at the University of California, San Diego, and that I don't think of myself as a constitutional conservative or, actually, any kind of conservative at all. I think of myself as a moderate, but part of the point is that what is "moderate" today in 2041 was considered extremely conservative 30 years ago. How that change came to be is the story.

I was a graduate student when Barack Obama was elected in 2008, and I voted for him—twice. I did not consider myself particularly political. I just shared the same views as those around me, and being in academia, those views were uniformly progressive. But, as what became a conservative insurgency against the progressive mainstream establishment developed over the decades that followed, I changed along with society. I, and most Americans, moved right. Gail Partridge and her fans did not.

"Do you want some milk?" asks Partridge. "It's raw."

"Kind of ironic, you drinking raw milk when that was one of

the flashpoints for so many people on the left turning right," I say, probing.

She scowls. "Nonsense. You know, five years ago a little girl in Kansas died drinking raw milk." She watches me, almost smiling. It's clear she's used the little girl anecdote before when the issue of government overreach and raw milk farmers comes back up. Almost 40 years of talk radio and Internet shows prepares you for any argument.

"So you were okay with the government jailing people for selling raw milk? How did you feel about the juror revolt against the prosecutions? That seemed an organic expression of opposition to authority. As a progressive, wouldn't that be something you would applaud?"

"A legitimate government has a right to exercise authority as it sees fit. The Supreme Court was absolutely right to put a stop to that juror misconduct. You can't change the system if short-sighted people are standing in your way."

"What about this government? This conservative government we have today?"

"I said a *legitimate* government," she sniffs.

Gail Partridge does not watch any media or popular entertainment besides other leftist hosts on her network. "The damn conservatives pop up on television and movies all the time now, and half the reporters seem to be looking to cover stories that hurt the progressive cause," she complains. "I liked it better when there was some balance in the media, and I could turn on the video feed without having to have any conservative crap come into my living room!"

She finds the constitutional conservative America of 2041 an alien and forbidding place.

"America may be fiscally better off, but it is morally bankrupt," she fumes as we sit in her penthouse apartment, looking out the window. "Patel makes a huge deal that he'll be paying off the national debt before the end of his term, but what about human need? Look out down there, down there in the streets. There are people hungry and cold down there right now. I don't care *how* they came to be hungry and cold. Maybe they didn't feel like working. Why should we judge them for that? I don't get why we should punish people for making different choices. It's fascist."

In three days, president-elect Rob Patel will be sworn in, and now Gail Partridge must prepare for another three-hour show devoted to venting her frustration at the new world she has found herself living in. I thank her for the raw milk and her time and prepare to leave. She walks me to the door and pushes the button to open it.

"I still don't understand how we got here," she says, sounding resigned. "I don't think we ever even saw the conservatives coming."

1

THE LONG MARCH

"We Never Really Had a Plan Except to Resist"

Just 28 years ago, as Barack Obama began his final term in office, and with the Tea Party success of 2010 considered merely a blip in leftism's relentless advance, conservatism appeared to be at its nadir in every arena of society. America, it appeared, had been "fundamentally transformed" into a poorer, less free, shadow of its former self.

Conservatism, the establishment agreed, was doomed.

But in 2041, the individualistic, free market ideology of constitutional conservatism rules in every major sphere of society. Progressivism is isolated and mocked. The most pronounced changes are outside of politics—constitutional conservatives are firmly established within the culture. In the media, in academia, the world of entertainment, and in everyday life, constitutional conservatism is—astonishingly to those over 40—the dominant paradigm. It is the cultural default, while its enemy, progressivism, is at best mocked as an archaic curiosity but more often scorned as a failed ideology of petty tyrants and elitist hypocrites. On television, it is the progressives who frequently find themselves the butt of jokes—and the conservatives are often the heroes.

This change did not simply happen. It was decades in the making, the result of a conscious and dedicated effort by constitutional conservatives to retake their country from the purveyors of progressivism. But it was not merely a political effort. Winning more political offices was a necessary, but not sufficient, goal. It was the culture that had grown to promote progressivism that would have to change.

It did not happen quickly. It faced many setbacks. But like Chairman Mao when he was forced to move his communist forces across China to escape destruction, it ended in victory.

Call it the constitutional conservatives' Long March.

■ ■ ■

Rob Patel (President-Elect)

It is hard to imagine any American who has managed to avoid learning president-elect Robert Manuel Patel's life story. In fact, in the last election his opponent famously sputtered in frustration, "He's nothing but biography!" But, of course, that sold Rob Patel well short. A savvy political operator who understood how it resonated, he ensured his uniquely American story was front and center throughout the campaign. Combined with his unapologetic conservatism, it helped earn him a 60 percent popular vote landslide.

The president-elect agreed to meet me the day before the inauguration in his suite of rooms in the Ritz-Carlton in Washington, DC. Security was tight—as always, the Secret Service was tracking multiple threats, many from leftists enraged at his plans to push forward the conservative policies of his two predecessors. They know better than to ignore the profound frustration of the disenfranchised left in light of the assassination attempt on the vice president in 2039 by a pair of self-described anarcho-socialists from Yale Law School. If one had not accidentally shot himself in the toe with his pistol, it might have ended in tragedy rather than farce.

Patel welcomes me and offers me coffee. The ostentatious appointments of the Presidential Suite seem to embarrass him. "We fought against people who were devoted to the trapping of power," he says. "And look at me now, in here, in the Ritz-Carlton! We need to keep reminding ourselves where we came from or we'll become the establishment." It's an illuminating analysis from a successor to 16 years of conservative rule—in many ways, the constitutional conservatives still see themselves as outsiders.

We sit, him on an overstuffed chair and me on the sofa, and he begins . . .

I was a young man out of college with a ton of student debt in 2012. I don't know—maybe $120,000, which was serious money then. I voted for Barack Obama because I really thought that government should and would take care of me. I thought it would care *for* me. After all, my teachers had taught me that all through my years in school. But then I got out into the real world, and there was nothing. No jobs, just lots of student loan debt weighing me down. It was the same for most of my friends.

Hope and change, Obama promised us, but all I saw was despair and decline. Yet as bad as the economy was, and it was really bad, the real problem was inside me. Like many in my generation, I had internalized a lot of the values and ideas of an American culture that had gone off track. I didn't yet have

27

the tools to succeed. I think liberals liked people like me being that way.

I tried and tried to get a job in my field, marketing, and no one was hiring. I remember talking to one employer and kind of *demanding* to know why he wouldn't give me a job, like he *owed* me a job. The guy looked at me, shook his head, and asked why he should hire anyone now when he couldn't be sure the government wouldn't put some new regulation or tax on him next year. He told me he didn't know how much I was going to cost from month to month because of all the things the government was doing to "help" me, and that's why I wasn't getting a job. It really opened my eyes, or rather, started to.

When I finally got a job with an energy company out in Montana, my eyes were opened even wider. I was working very hard but my taxes were increasing, while more and more of my peers were sitting around doing nothing (often by choice) and getting paid for it!

Then the final straw came when the Obama administration's EPA essentially banned fracking and I got laid off. I figured out that the only people liberals cared about were their fellow elitist progressives in Manhattan, Hollywood, Chicago, and DC. People like me were collateral damage, acceptable losses, for making their dreams come true.

I registered as a Republican while working at a McDonald's.

Colonel Jeremy Denton, US Army (Ret.) (Insurgency Expert)

This gruff former Army War College instructor and Iraq/Afghanistan veteran lives outside of Atlanta, north of his old haunts at Fort Benning. He wears a .45 on his hip, largely as a political statement. His specialty on active duty was counterinsurgency warfare, but his passion was conservative politics. It was only after leaving active service that he got personally involved, but that did not keep him from turning his professional eye toward what was happening from the outside. As we talk, he seems to shift personas—from Army officer to college professor to barstool smart-ass and back again.

As we enjoy a cold Dos Equis on his porch, the colonel observes, "Now, insurgency is not a perfect metaphor for what happened. There was no real fighting, though I think there could have been if things happened differently. I don't even want to think about that. But I see so many parallels to an insurgency that I think using it as the paradigm is the best way to understand what happened since 2009."

The best reason for embarking on a conservative insurgency was the fact that we did not have a whole lot of other strategic options. We didn't have a strong, organized majority that could try to push through what we wanted politically, and we had no real infrastructure to do it in the social and cultural spheres. With the eight-inch artillery that was the liberal mainstream media out there ready to call a fire mission in on any concentration of conservative power, there was no other viable strategic option. It wasn't a conscious decision, of course—it just happened organically. We never really had a plan except to resist. That's pretty much the best way for an insurgency to happen.

Look back at where we were at our low point in early 2013. Even if the political correlation of forces was different—say, if Romney had won in 2012 and perhaps the GOP had retaken the Senate—we still would probably have had to choose insurgency. Romney's primary asset was that he wasn't a liberal—well, at least that he wasn't a liberal anymore—but he was certainly no constitutional conservative. He wasn't a bad guy. He just wasn't

29

committed to the cause. He got a lot of support from the kind of milquetoast Republican who would bloviate about "working together" and "compromising" and "doing the job the American people sent us here to do" as a prelude to sticking real conservatives in the back. We would have had that fight with them if he had won; turns out, we had to have it anyway before we could really take on the liberals.

So even if we had Obama out of the White House, we would not have had a true constitutional conservative in it. And just because we might have had a Republican president would have done nothing for what was arguably the bigger problem conservatives faced, the liberal culture.

Say we had Romney and a GOP House and a GOP Senate and even a stronger GOP-inclined Supreme Court . . . so? At the end of the day, that would have been just a temporary correlation of forces. Parties change quickly, but culture . . . the culture changes slowly, and its impact dwarfs the transitory changes in Washington.

We conservatives had very little hold on the culture, and little combat power to retake it. Even with the political reins of power in our hands, the culture would remain progressive, incubating the virus of collectivist thought like monkeys in the jungle provide a reservoir for the Ebola virus. I like that—liberalism as a political Ebola virus!

Anyway, liberalism would just sit there, in the bastions of cultural progressivism—academia, the arts, the media, entertainment, and some sectors of the nonprofit and religious communities—waiting for a chance to spread once again.

No, even if we were stronger, our strategic choice would have to have been an insurgency. We couldn't hit the strongholds of cultural progressivism head-on, not without causing massive resistance and a cultural fight we'd have had little or no chance of winning. Remember, they wanted to be victims, to be rebels—we'd be throwing them in the locally sourced, organic briar patch.

No, we needed to infiltrate them, quietly, stealthily, even as we cut off their subsidy money and negated their influence from the outside. We needed to go slowly, embarking upon the same kind of long-term campaign that led that crop of aging hippies and Viet Cong–hugging creeps to positions of authority and influence.

We had to destroy them from the inside by turning the culture conservative over time. We had to be stealthy and take advantage of our relatively few tactical advantages. And the only way to do that was through an insurgency.

Now, the strength of any insurgency is that it is decentralized. Conversely, the weakness of any insurgency is that it is decentralized. That's the conundrum of insurgency.

A traditional military unit succeeds because the commander can use his force's centralized command structure to synchronize efforts and focus combat power at decisive points within the battlespace. "Battlespace" is the replacement term for "battlefield"—there's a whole wing of the Pentagon devoted to making up new words for perfectly good old words! They made up "battlespace" to recognize not just the three-dimensional nature of physical warfare but the intangible cyber/electronic and social arenas as well.

Anyway, a traditional commander has a centralized command and control system that lets him make everyone do what he wants them to do and go where he wants them to go to hit the other side all at the same time.

But insurgents have trouble doing that. Why? Because they aren't centralized. Their chain of command is not so rigid—local leaders have significant power and may not answer to one overall commander. Logistically, they have trouble moving across the battlespace. Their problem is one of concentration—it's hard for an insurgency to concentrate forces at a particular point in time and space in significant numbers.

Concentration allows you to focus combat power at one place for a maximum effect. Let me give you an example. You have 100 guys each with a pistol that has an effective range of, say, 50 meters. Each of them is 50 meters apart. So, the greatest number of your guys who can concentrate fire on one spot is three at a time unless you can move them, right?

But if you can coordinate, say, 20 of those guys to move to within 50 meters of a spot, you can then concentrate 20 guns on that spot. If you really want to kill something, have more guns concentrating fire on it. So, that's concentration.

Now, if there were no downside to concentration, we would concentrate forces all the time. But concentrating your forces in one place is risky. It gives the other side a target! That's why insurgents, at least smart ones, don't concentrate their forces until they absolutely have to, and then only at the last minute. They avoid a force-on-force fight. The traditional military has a huge advantage because it is designed to concentrate overwhelming force quickly and efficiently.

But this challenge for insurgents is also one of their greatest strengths. Insurgents are rarely concentrated, which is good, because traditional military forces are designed to smash concentrated enemy forces—they *like* it when an insurgent concentrates his forces because then they can mass their full combat power on the insurgents and inflict maximum damage.

32 Think of a traditional military as a sledgehammer and the insurgent as a mosquito. Yeah, if the sledgehammer hits the

mosquito it's "Adios, bug." But what if there is a *swarm* of mosquitoes? Then, perhaps, the sledgehammer is a suboptimal weapon system for the job.

Now let's apply that concept to a peaceful ideological struggle. Back in 2013, the liberal establishment was that traditional force. It was big, and its power was daunting. It occupied most of the government. It had heavy artillery in the form of the mainstream media. It was totally supported by the cultural left in Hollywood and academia. We constitutional conservatives simply did not have the firepower to take it on face-to-face back then. When we tried, we lost—look at the shutdown fight of October 2013. We lost because we provided a target and the entire liberal establishment, aided and abetted by the GOP moderates, was able to focus its fire on us.

So, the answer was not to concentrate our forces to give them a target they could crush with one blow. Instead, we needed to be millions of little mosquitoes, each taking a bit of blood out of the flabby liberal lummox swinging that sledgehammer.

Sandy Crawford (Conservative Activist)

The long-time conservative activist and organizer, now a senior fellow at the Breitbart Institute, still likes to fight. However, today she finds herself in the unusual (for her) position of defending the status quo. It's clear, though, that her true calling is really being an insurgent, of fighting outnumbered and outgunned.

We had no real choice about how we were going to fight back. The Republican establishment seemed content to lose. The media was totally against us. Everywhere you looked in the culture—movies, TV, the arts—constitutional conservatives

33

were the enemy. We were almost completely locked out of academia. They were attacking everywhere our values were strong and defied the liberal zeitgeist—religion, business, and the military. So doing it ourselves was the only way to go.

It wasn't like we planned it. We just understood that we needed to use our individual skills and talents, and that we couldn't write off any part of the culture anymore. We had technology too, which gave us the power to organize and exponentially increase our voice. But what we really had was an understanding that progressivism under these administrations represented a real threat, and that we couldn't just ignore what was happening and hope it would be taken care of somehow, by someone else. We learned that we had to fight even as we were living our lives, and that our careers, our political action, and social interactions—well, we couldn't pretend these were separate from our conservative beliefs. So everything we did supported the fight.

Ted Jindal (Technology Consultant)

Ted Jindal (no relation to the former vice president) was very familiar with the state of play for conservatives on the technology front during the Obama and Hillary years. As a young technology expert, he was there on the front lines while the insurgency struggled against the Democrats' high-tech superiority.

I was a new media guy for the Romney 2012 campaign—naturally, I told them to pound sand when they tried to get me back in 2016. It was awful. The GOP knew nothing about technology or new media. They paid consultants huge bucks for these nearly useless systems that were essentially designed to send an e-mail to people saying, "Don't forget to vote." And they couldn't even pull that off. They had no concept, and in 2016 it wasn't much better. Technology was just a buzzword and a scapegoat. It was like, "Uh, I think we need more technology and social media. Go buy some!" But, outside of the candidates and the party, conservatives were starting to figure things out. I soon figured out that I was seeing things precisely backwards.

By the teens, there were all of these new media tools using the Internet. You had your Twitter, your Facebook, blogs, video blogs, and podcasts. Constitutional conservatives were all over them. They would just start doing things on their own and either get an audience or not get an audience and move onto something else. It was totally organic. It was the free market we always talked about in action before our eyes. Naturally, we didn't see that.

Of course, I came from the business side, very old school. As a new media guy—which I guess is old media today—I was totally wrong in my own outlook, and yet I was still light-years ahead of other folks working on this for our side. The thing that I needed to get into my head, and that took me a long time to get my head around, was that this wasn't a phenomenon we could control and direct.

In the campaigns, we tried to coordinate things, to set the agenda ourselves by forcing our messages to the forefront. But even to the extent we could round up these free agents to try and coordinate them, they refused to be coordinated. Have you ever tried to get a mailing list of 200 key Twitter, Facebook, and blog influencers to follow your directions and talk about what you wanted talked about that day? Forget it. I would try to issue them talking points for the news cycle—I had this vision that I could somehow synchronize them into talking about what we on the campaigns had decided was important. Well, they just ignored us and did their own thing, or they told us to buzz off. And they didn't use the word "buzz."

We were tremendously frustrated that we couldn't control the messaging. There were messages out there all right, often very powerful ones for our side, but we couldn't control them.

What I initially missed was that this was a crowdsourcing phenomenon. Instead of trying to force my chosen messages to resonate, the messages that really resonated—the memes—would rise naturally from the confluence of the new media sources out there in the web. The good stuff, the powerful constitutional conservative messages that really worked for us, bubbled up and got big without some central controller picking and choosing them. In other words, the good stuff would take off and go viral on its own.

We started doing a lot better with our messaging when we stopped trying to tell constitutional conservatives what the message du jour was and started listening to them tell *us* what it was.

David Chang (Conservative Media Host)

In 2041, America's number-one conservative satellite/web talk show host is David Chang. Chang, a gay conservative evangelical Christian who often spars with his conservative atheist cohost Timmy Tyler, is often called "the Rush Limbaugh of our generation." He recalls how the elite liberal mindset was simply intolerable and how he fought back. Chang is a 2015 Harvard Law School graduate who first made a name for himself when he forced the school to readmit him after expelling him for "hate speech" for wondering aloud in class, "How can any gay American be part of the fraud that is progressivism? You know that it was the progressive's brothers the Nazis who pinned pink triangles to us and put us in camps, right?"

Liberalism was flabby. It was tired and bloated, a worn-out giant bereft of ideas and ideals. Maybe, at some point in the past, liberals believed in something. But by 2020, you never heard about "bleeding heart" liberals anymore because you needed to have a heart to have it bleed.

They no longer bought their own nonsense—they just mouthed the words. And we had all heard the words and phrases so often, they lost any meaning even to the suckers who believed them before they became clichés.

"War on Women." "Racism." "Fair share." It was all crap. It was all a scam.

Liberalism's corruption was so complete they didn't even try to hide it anymore. Crusader for the little guy Al Gore made a fortune off the global warming swindle—it's still getting colder 30 years on!—and then he doubled it selling his Current TV network to the oil sheiks of the Middle East for a stack of petrodollars. He didn't even bother to explain it. And no one on the left bothered to comment. Why? Because everyone who had bothered to pay attention—the politicians, the pundits, the media mavens, the cocktail party intelligentsia—all knew that liberalism was just a crock of bullshit.

The Obama campaign won reelection in 2012 based not on "Hope and Change" but on slander and lies. Hillary Clinton didn't even pretend. She was right out front—it was about greed. Vote for her and she would steal from her opponents and give you a cut via entitlements.

But Americans aren't a cynical people. I talk to them and with them every day. They are actually very idealistic, and the Constitution embodies that idealism. They started to see the truth, that liberalism was nothing more than a racket designed to spread

37

the spoils in the form of money and power among a small group of elitists on the coasts, in the faculty lounges, and in DC. The poor, well, they got a few scraps—not enough to live like free men and women, but enough to buy their votes in exchange for their dignity. The liberals knew it. We conservatives certainly knew it. Our challenge was getting the *rest* of America to know it. We wanted all Americans to internalize this truth the way that popular culture had led them to internalize the bizarre lie that conservatives are repressed sexaphobes who obeyed that Pat Robertson guy and wanted to ban fun in all its forms. That sure as hell wasn't me, and it sure wasn't the constitutional conservatives I knew.

Brad Fields (Insurance Salesman)

Fields is a self-described "regular guy," having never previously held office or been involved in politics, but having been drawn into the insurgency during the Obama administration as things began to fall apart. You get the impression that he considers politics a bother, that he would prefer doing just about anything else. In fact, he only becomes truly excited discussing Clemson football—his office is decked with team memorabilia. As for his role in the insurgency, he talks about it as if having to get involved was an inconvenience. You get the distinct impression he did so only reluctantly, and only because he saw he had no other choice.

Do you think I dreamed of selling insurance as a kid growing up? Could anything be sadder? I wanted to be a lawyer, but when I finished college I was already in $50,000 of debt, and there was no way I was going to spend three years and $250,000 to be an unemployed shyster. But grad school seemed my only option. There were no jobs—none—for people like me. I poured coffee at a Starbucks in the 2010s, fetching lattes for liberal snobs. Of course, I was liberal too then, I guess. I didn't really care about politics. I just wanted to do my thing, watch the game on the weekend, and drink some beers.

See this scar? It used to be a tattoo of the Chinese character for luck, or so I was told. I thought it was so cool. I was too stupid to see that I was wrong for a long time. I was also too stupid to see that I was wrong about liberalism until I realized that it was being built on my back and I wasn't getting squat— except for being called a racist or a sexist or whatever during our company diversity seminars. So I was almost happy to get a gig selling health insurance, a perfect fit for a guy with a bachelor's degree in communications, whatever that was. I'm still not sure what I got out of college except an exhausted liver.

Anyway, my job was to try to explain Obamacare to these small business owners and individuals. It was a nightmare. It was a total train wreck, and I remember wondering why the Democrats resisted any effort to fix even the stupidest provisions. Initially I blamed the Republicans because, well, everything was always the Republicans' fault, right? But after a while, I started to figure out the truth—and seeing my lazy classmates who weren't working living off government money about as well as I was living off of money I earned and then paid out in taxes certainly helped.

Obamacare started falling apart right from the beginning. I was cancelling long-time customers and all I could offer were these new policies for more money with higher deductibles. People would ask me why this was happening, and one day I just lost it and said, "It's the damn liberals. They never should have screwed with it." That's when I realized I was a constitutional conservative.

Ashley Hampton (Reluctant Conservative Activist)

A Portland antique compact disc store owner ("You're going to hate me for being a Portland cliché, but I really do prefer CD sound quality and texture to newer music delivery media") and self-described ex-liberal, Hampton found herself under enormous peer pressure when she began asking uncomfortable questions about progressive premises.

How liberal was I? Oh gosh, totally. If there was a liberal cliché, I was it. I was against racism, sexism, homophobia, lookism, fatism—everything—and, of course, I saw them everywhere. The Republicans, especially the Tea Party people, now they were just awful. I hated them. They were the worst human beings on earth. Worse than Nazis, who at that time I still thought were right-wingers.

Of course, I had never actually met any Tea Partiers—or Tea Baggers, as we liked to call them—but I was liberal and I didn't need to actually know someone to know that I was better and more moral than him.

I was really into feminism. I saw patriarchy everywhere. I initially responded to the liberal outreach to women like me—they seemed to be telling me that as a young, single woman, liberalism was going to take care of me. There was this cartoon character, Julia, that the liberals used in the Obama campaign. This Julia, at every juncture of her life, was getting something from the government. Cradle to grave, the government was taking care of her.

But after a while this had started to bother me at some level, because it seemed that as a feminist I shouldn't be relying on others. To me, feminism was, and is, about finding the power within myself to think and do for myself. I didn't need a man to support me, but then the liberals were telling me that I needed them. My friends didn't seem bothered by it, and I kind of put it aside, but it seemed weird to me.

I thought liberalism was about freedom. Really, I did. I just hadn't thought about it critically yet. But then even more of these things started coming out that kind of puzzled me. There was the NSA surveillance thing—the government was listening in to telephone calls and tracking people's Internet use. That really bothered me, and I remember getting grief because I blamed Obama. I mean, he was the president when they were doing this, so who was I supposed to blame? Well, evidently Bush, because some of it started under him. But I couldn't understand why my liberal friends were letting Obama off the hook for not stopping it. It seemed really clear to me.

I started getting uncomfortable thoughts about the hypocrisy I was seeing on my own side. Liberals lied to us about health care, but that was okay because health care was really important. Since when was lying okay? Then you'd have liberal politicians being harassers and abusers, but we were supposed to blame the women because the men were too important to the liberal cause to hold accountable. What?

I would see my liberal friends use the most vicious, hateful, sexist words about conservative women. I was no Sarah Palin fan, but one day this feminist bookstore owner called her the "c word" at a reading and I stood up and said, "As a feminist, I can't accept you using that term about another woman." I got booed, and the woman hissed at me, "That conservative bitch isn't a woman!" The feminists all clapped. It was crazy to me.

I would have loved to see their faces when President Marlowe appointed Ambassador Palin to the United Nations and she told those crooks and thugs to shape up or ship out of New York City!

I knew something had changed in me. I hadn't changed any of my core principles. I think the thing is—and I saw this with a lot of liberals who became constitutional conservatives—is that I actually believed in all that stuff about treating people fairly and equally and about civil rights and so forth. But a lot of liberals seemed to think those principles were only important as long as they helped liberalism. When they didn't help, they abandoned them. The liberals were leaving me, not vice versa.

I was a big pro-choice supporter, but I never thought abortion was right for me. I wasn't going to judge others, but for me, I just wasn't going to have one. Then I got pregnant, and I naturally decided I was going to keep the baby. I thought that being pro-choice meant that I had a right to choose, but when I said why I chose to have my daughter even though I was very poor and fairly young—and suggested that other people should try to do the same, even if inconvenient—you'd think I had just burned a cross. I guess they were all for choice if you chose their way.

Suddenly, I had feminists telling me that I was somehow betraying feminist principles by having the baby. It seemed like it was important to them that I atone for not being more than just pro-choice. They had forgiven me for defending Sarah Palin, but I finally got kicked out of the feminist bookstore reading club for good for that.

And it wasn't just the feminists. This environmentalist feminist I knew named Gaia Borgnine—I don't know if that was her real name—actually came up to me in my shop and told me having a child was an "Earthcrime." I asked whether I was going to be arrested by the "Earthcops," and she said, "If I had my way, you would be!"

These people were nuts. And dangerous.

I started reading and learning about the people I had always held in contempt. It took a while, but after finding that liberal "freedom" was really no freer than the caricature of conservatism I had grown up believing in, I committed the ultimate act of defiance. I started my own Tea Party group, and I used the name "Tea Party" explicitly to confront the haters. And there were plenty. Of course, being Portland, I emphasized that the tea was locally sourced.

2

GUERRILLA POLITICS

"I Felt Like a Viet Cong Guy in a Polo Shirt and Dockers"

Success in the political realm was not sufficient for victory, but it was necessary for victory. Conservative politicians were under fire not only from the Democrats but from establishment Republicans, as well as the media. Not yet strong enough to pass any initiatives on their own, they moved into the guerrilla mode of defeating their opponents' attempt to govern. Using spectacle to highlight establishment weakness, and choosing fights where they had a good chance of winning, constitutional conservatives began to exercise a power beyond their relatively limited size. Leveraging grassroots enthusiasm and making use of the sanctuary of the states (where much of the work of the conservative comeback took place), conservatives began to shape the battlefield for eventual victory.

■ ■ ■

Tony "Gator" McCoy (Chief Advisor to President Carrie Marlowe)

Gator McCoy played football at Florida State, where he majored in cheap beer and right-wing activism. A shattered knee put him on the sidelines, but his keen, competitive drive found a new outlet: politics. Starting out as a Sunshine State campaign prodigy winning elections that the establishment had written off, he built a wide network of contacts within the constitutional conservative movement. The network paid off when Carrie Marlowe brought him on-board to manage her run for governor in 2018 and her eventual run for the White House in 2024.

It's only 10:30 in the morning when Gator guides me out to his back porch and cracks a Budweiser. I decline his third wife's offer of a brew—at 30, she is half his age—and take a seat. Gator kicks off his flip-flops and puts up his feet.

After the 2012 election, the weenies of the GOP started looking around for an excuse for their screw-ups—of course, their defeat couldn't be because of their milquetoast policies and Beltway worldview. Oh no, it had to be, uh . . . who? Why, those conservatives! Oh, and also a lack of inclusiveness—which, of course, just happened to dovetail with their own preconceived, establishment notions about immigration. They blamed everyone and everything but themselves.

There was something to be said for expanding the GOP voter base, but it wasn't being said by the establishment. Their big contribution to the discussion was the bright idea that if us crazy constitutional conservatives would simply adopt the Beltway consensus on immigration, Latinos would come rushing into the

GOP from their Democrat home because, well, uh . . . See, they never had a good answer.

Oh, I raised hell with them. I was challenging their shaky premises and asking simple questions like "Why do you believe that is true?" when I was supposed to sit back and let the geniuses who brought us winners like McCain and Romney tell me what to think.

No friggin' way!

Florida was always a big melting pot, so I know something about appealing to different voting blocs. I tried to tell them that networking was not about taking a look at a census spreadsheet and pointing to a category like "Hispanics" and saying, "Let's target them!" Leaving aside that "Latinos," "Hispanics," or whatever they were being called are not some sort of homogenous voting bloc, the whole thing was totally *un*conservative.

We conservatives weren't about appealing to people based on where their grandfather came from. We were supposed to be appealing to them because they love the values embodied in our Constitution!

I tried to tell the establishment, "Hey, we aren't liberals!" They wouldn't listen. Too dug in. Too entrenched. Too stupid.

I quit my GOP establishment job in DC and went home to Tampa. I found good candidates in tough races and helped them win by running as constitutional conservatives. When I ran a campaign, from city council to president, I wanted to sneak in and steal the Democrat base. I wanted to come in under the cover of darkness and rob 'em blind. I felt like a Viet Cong guy in a polo shirt and Dockers.

But networking into groups we had ignored wasn't going to work if we tried to do it based on gimmicks like an amnesty

immigration bill. Seriously, where was the one "Latino" anywhere who had ever been caught on video saying, "Why yes, if
the GOP copies the Democrats on immigration I'll immediately
start voting Republican for some reason"?

Never happened before, and when they finally pushed it
through, it still didn't happen.

I got my candidates to aim at people who agreed with our
principles but who, because of habits associated with their race,
ethnicity, affinity, or whatever, would not support our Republican
candidates. And we needed to keep clear-eyed understanding of
what we meant by "principles." The nonsense about how Hispanics
were somehow inherently conservative because they are "pro-
family" and religious was the kind of fuzzy, half-assed thinking
our establishment overlords always confused with strategy.

You know who else is really, really religious? Black women.
Did you see a lot of black women voting Republican? You see
some doing it now, but it took work, not position papers from
DC think tanks. I kept saying, "Clichés aren't metrics, people!"

Our success came from trying to get people to join us not because of demographic factors but because they shared our constitutional conservative principles. They just didn't always know
it yet. I won campaigns because I showed them!

Jack Archer (Democratic Strategist)

The retired Democratic strategist is still bitter when he recalls how
the conservatives, left with nothing but a shaky grip on the House,
managed to hold off the efforts of the Democrats and their media
allies to crush them by cleverly avoiding traps and keeping focused on their objectives. In contrast to his old foe Gator McCoy,
Jack Archer sits alone in a New York City apartment writing up his

memoirs in the hope that they might be of use for liberals hoping to take power again someday. "It's not really an autobiography," he notes glumly. "It's more of a postmortem."

I hated those bastards. The conservatives didn't even pretend to respect their role or the processes of government. We couldn't break their hold on the House. Their states had gerrymandered very, very effectively, so it was structurally difficult to do anyway. We tried and tried, but they kept holding on, and that totally screwed our plans. And we were so focused on their rear guard in Washington that we missed them growing out in Middle America. I mean, occasionally we'd watch a governor's race in Colorado or Missouri for a little while, but then it'd be back to focusing on DC. What a huge mistake—they were growing like a cancer out in the states.

I'll be honest—we tried to make them into monsters. It worked for a while. Then the damn Republicans suddenly refused to cooperate. They stopped putting the same mush-mouthed, old white guy losers in front of the cameras as the voice of the party. They coordinated their talking points so we couldn't get any clips of backbenchers going off message. They got a bunch of conservative trial lawyers to come to DC and train their members on how to talk to people like human beings and to advocate effectively instead of make fools of themselves.

In other words, they got smart. Maybe they realized what we were doing. Maybe they figured out we were serious about making them extinct and taking the country left.

Still, after the shutdown thing at the end of 2013, we figured we'd just keep forcing them into confrontations and pummel them with our media. Yeah, it was our media—it knew what we wanted and was happy to help us. We already hung the "Tea

49

Party" label around the conservative senators like Ted Cruz, and the media was helping to make it radioactive.

Of course, the Obamacare fiasco derailed us. I thought we were going to be finished when millions of Americans woke up to find the Democrats lied to them and they were losing their plans and their doctors. But we got another chance. If those GOP idiots hadn't decided to push through amnesty in 2014, we would have been crushed and never restarted our momentum.

We played on their divisions in the GOP. We identified Republican moderates, and our media friends tried to get them to break ranks. They fell for it every time. There was this governor in New Jersey, Chris Christie, a big guy—he was always good for a slam on his party. Put a mic in front of his face and he'd trash the conservatives all day with a smile. We loved him. He probably could have been president, too, if he hadn't burned all his bridges, so to speak. He went to Iowa and got about 4 percent of the vote. Then he did the "sensible moderate spoiler thing" and got Hillary reelected in 2020. He just faded away.

But this was a serious fight. We were playing for keeps. We had this great idea about how we were just going to tear them up, wedge out the reasonable ones from the hard-core Tea Party types, and totally destroy the opposition. That's what we were after—I know we denied it, but we wanted to eliminate any opposition. We wanted the Republican Party dead, and there were a lot of Republicans who seemed willing to go along with it. It was the conservatives who wouldn't give up. They refused to die.

We tried to do what the damn conservatives have actually done to us today. I'm kind of sorry, you know, that we threw all the norms of collegiality and loyalty in opposition out the door, because as soon as the GOP took power it used the same tactics against us. Court packing, executive orders, eliminating the filibuster—we threw out the rules, and then the conservatives came and shoved them up our asses. And now we're the ones who are almost extinct.

I hated those bastards.

Tamara Hayes Smith (Professor/Activist)

A Yale political science professor, Professor Smith was one of the first of the new wave of conservative academics to grudgingly receive tenure at the Ivy League schools after a combination of public opinion, alumni activism, political pressure regarding federal funding, and structural changes created by new technology forced liberal academia to diversify.

Yale is one of the few colleges to still use the "traditional method," with resident students undertaking a four-year curriculum with entirely live professors in both lecture and seminar settings. "I am grateful I have the luxury of face-to-face interaction with students," she says. "Few academics do anymore. They can blame economics, technology, and themselves for that."

Her students are the cream of the crop, with the school using its endowment to pay the costs of those who can't afford the $350,000 per year tuition and room and board costs. With the end of government student loan programs and new laws requiring schools to spend a portion of their endowments annually, both Professor Smith's students and the school are very focused on making the most of what is, today, a rare educational opportunity.

Professor Smith's office is plastered with campaign signs from the last three decades, a graphic lesson in history for the students who crowd in during her weekly office hours to learn from the foremost academic scholar of the constitutional conservative movement. I catch up with her as she talks to a few of them one winter afternoon.

The conservatives shook up the establishment because they came into the political process totally focused on their core beliefs, not on the perks of power, and they felt little or no allegiance to the "institutions" or their processes. The GOP establishment was slow to realize that these constitutional conservatives were serious about their goals. You can't buy off committed ideologues. The establishment politicians were used to people playing conservative at home and then coming to DC and being co-opted.

But the conservatives arrived feeling not a part of Washington or sharing its Beltway worldview, and they felt no loyalty to the status quo. The establishment couldn't control them, so it decided that it had to try to crush them.

We need to understand the establishment perspective and how disruptive this was to the status quo. Understand that political power was not the be-all and end-all of the conservative movement. This was a fight across every part of society, and while political power was necessary, it was not sufficient. Conservatives saw that, and because personal political power was not their goal, the usual carrots and sticks of Washington—the proverbial cocktail party invitations—didn't influence them.

This baffled and frightened the establishment of both parties. This is why the insurgents were painted as crazy, or "whacko birds" in the immortal characterization of Senator John McCain.

Until the conservative movement built up enough raw political power, its members needed to avoid decisive fights on the establishment's terms. They didn't always do that. In the fall of 2013, the insurgents led by Senator Ted Cruz forced a government shutdown. The establishment Republicans hated it and joined in with the liberal establishment to beat them down. The establishment still had overwhelming power (including the liberal media) that it could use to crush the insurgents when they picked a fight.

Barack Obama, of course, loved it. He sought out crises—he loved them. He thought he would win when he pushed things to the brink, and too often he did. But just weeks later the disaster of Obamacare became all too undeniable, first with the website failing and then with the realization that the liberals had outright lied about what the law would do to regular people's medical insurance policies. That was a key event, and the insurgents were there pointing out the disaster that liberalism had wrought.

Many establishment Republicans saw this in the context of short-term advantage, and it was a short-term advantage. It was enough to hold the House in 2014 despite the amnesty debacle, but Hillary Clinton would still win the 2016 election. The insurgents saw it as something more, the end of the beginning of the fall of liberalism rather than the beginning of the end of liberalism. Obamacare would fuel their critique of the establishment's Beltway-based thinking as part of a long-term project to remake American culture.

The insurgents learned not to fight just to fight, but to fight to win. Because they lacked raw political power, they learned to be careful about where they let themselves be engaged. Some felt that they were insufficiently aggressive, and mistakenly lumped them in with the establishment GOP mandarins who were reticent because, below the surface, they did not support the change the insurgents sought. Their statist ox was being gored too.

The insurgents learned to make absolutely sure that the situation and correlation of forces favored them greatly before consenting to engage in battle. Simply put, they picked their fights after the 2013 government shutdown. They understood that they had no solid allies—the establishment GOP, given the choice between conservative change that would disrupt their power and position, would support the status quo when push came to shove.

And it was quite frustrating, not only to the establishment that—try as it might—just could not stamp out these stubborn insurgents because the insurgents would not let them leverage the establishment's full weight against them, but to the insurgents themselves. The conservatives wanted to fight—they were hungry for the chance to take their progressive opponents down a peg or twenty. But the goal wasn't merely to fight. Fighting was a tactic, not a goal. The goal was to win in the long run by winning over the culture. So they had to walk away from most fights, and that was very frustrating for a furious grassroots base.

It was especially frustrating for conservative politicians trying to make clear to their own rank and file that avoiding disadvantageous engagements was a strategic choice, not a lack of will to win. Just saying it wasn't enough—the conservatives needed wins to keep from being demoralized. The insurgents needed to look for situations where they were likely to win—even little victories helped keep morale up when there were setbacks, like the election and reelection of Hillary Clinton.

The Obamacare rollout debacle was a fortuitous one—it came right on the heels of most of the Washington, DC, punditocracy pronouncing the Tea Party dead. One note on the term "Tea Party"—that label was Alinskyed by the left and by the establishment of both parties into an all-purpose enemy upon which they could focus their efforts. It was an attempt to manufacture a single, identifiable, and tangible opponent to destroy. But there was no Tea Party. It was a chimera. Certainly, a few organizations used the name, but there was no single entity that could be destroyed. The establishment turned its full power against this so-called "Tea Party" and poisoned it with normal Americans—but there was nothing there. The conservative insurgency was not bound to the fate of the "Tea Party." The establishment ended up defeating only a label while its actual opponent was growing stronger.

It became clear to the insurgents that they had to force the GOP to act during Obama's remaining time in office to defeat his plans, mostly pushed through via executive orders and by gimmicks like ending the filibuster, while setting the stage to enact its own goals. They wisely gave up on trying to govern.

They hated it when establishment GOP politicians went on Sunday morning television shows—Sunday morning was when they ran all the boring political programs at the time—and started babbling about "governing." They realized that the Republicans needed to forget about "governing" and try to stay alive as a party. They wanted to let Obama "govern," if he could, which meant let him pay the consequences for his policies. The Obamacare rollout fiasco was a great example—and the conservatives had to work hard to prevent establishment Republicans from bailing Obama out from the consequences of his actions in the name of "good governance."

Every time the GOP tried to reform something or improve something, they either got skewered by the media or helped Obama avoid the fallout of his own actions. The conservatives preferred to focus on the only goal that mattered: destroying the progressive movement. That meant letting Obama and Clinton fail.

55

Sandy Crawford (Conservative Activist)

The Breitbart Institute has a bar with 23 beers on tap. This is just one of the ways in which it attempts to honor its namesake, whose love of the occasional quaff was almost as great as his love of battling the liberal establishment. Sandy and I sit at a table in the corner watching the young staffers gather to blow off steam after another week of hard work fighting for control of the culture.

I was not born into the movement. I came into it because, well, I was a thinking human being and I hated the conformity and lying I saw the liberals around me get wrapped up in. I started out generally liberal, so I kind of knew how they thought—or didn't, as the case may be. But I got the appeal of liberalism, which some of my fellow cons never did. I understood why someone might choose to be liberal. I didn't agree with the rationale, but I got the thought process. There was a security in giving up your autonomy in return for vague assurances that you would be taken care of. Many of us in the constitutional conservative movement understood, because many of us were ex-liberals. I think it gave us an advantage in appealing to regular Americans.

I got active in the movement after college and bounced around various organizations and institutions doing conservative activist work. In college, I started out an English major, which meant I was set to be a lawyer or a barista. I ended up with a degree in poli sci and marketing. Both were useful down the road.

I understood the cultural challenge, but I wanted to work on the political side. Pretty quickly I saw that to win—and we did not win much at first—we needed to fight on our terms, where we could do the most damage to not just Democrats but liberals in general.

56

Now, most professional politicians are terrible politicians. I don't know how they get elected. So many of them are lawyers, but they can barely make an argument. They're awful advocates and they have no sense of strategy. We tried to advise them on how to do it better, so that the constitutional conservative message would get out and so they wouldn't step on their stuff talking about insane things, like their personal rape theories. Geez, I still don't know what possessed some of those guys, but some lib reporter would ask them about rape and they would go on a two-minute monologue that made them look like idiots from the Dark Ages. It seemed like it was irresistible to them—no matter how many times you'd say to them, "If someone asks about rape, tell him you're against it," they would just keep talking. It still baffles me.

So, we saw ourselves as a resource helping constitutional conservatives at every level with articulating their views and organizing for success. I worked for candidates from senators down to, literally, a dogcatcher. Really, a dogcatcher. I'm not even sure which organization it was—I think it was before I moved to FreedomWorks—that sent me to help this conservative candidate for director of animal control for some county in Colorado. These pushy liberal vegan activists were trying to take over the job, which is an important job in a semirural area. I mean, it was important enough that it was an elected office there. Anyway, this guy was a manager at a grocery store and a Tea Party activist who had started off working to recall some gun-banning state senators. Well, he saw this going on, and he liked animals, so he ran, but he didn't know anything. I got sent out to help him, and he ended up winning.

Sure, dogcatcher is a pretty minor office, but here's the thing. It was a stepping-stone. We were building a constitutional conservative farm team. He got elected dogcatcher in 2018. He's a conservative congressman now.

We tried to get our candidates to think strategically. The challenge was that the Tea Party brought in a lot of amateurs, people with no political experience. But that was also a good thing because we could start fresh with them and not have to waste time breaking bad habits. This was definitely not true about the pros, or *alleged* pros. They thought they knew everything, which was true—if you were talking about getting your butt kicked by liberals. They were experts at that.

We tried to get them to avoid issues that required compromise, which they resisted. They would talk about this nebulous need to "solve problems," not realizing that you weren't going to solve any problems while liberals were in control. You were only going to put off the final collapse of liberalism. Our job during the Obama and Clinton years was not "good government." It was destroying the liberal cancer plaguing our government at every level.

We pushed them to choose smaller issues that we could win, that would embarrass the opposition or at least jam a wedge between their key constituencies. The best issues led to concrete wins for us.

For example, we tried to get them to make sure that any kind of "gun violence" proposal included amendments that required liberals to go on record supporting or opposing the individual right to keep and bear arms. If we won, we strengthened the right to keep and bear arms. If we lost, we at least outed the liberals who liked to pretend to be protecting gun rights for the benefit of the voters back home in red states. We looked for these win-wins.

There were a lot of old white guys who were the face of conservatism. Now, I like old white guys. My dad was an old white guy. But there was a lot more to the constitutional conservative movement than old white guys. Hell, the original Tea Party—okay, not the *original* original Tea Party—was led primarily by women. There was nothing wrong with who they were. It just presented a distorted view of who we were as a movement.

So, we pushed local groups and candidates to put females out there to talk about how women benefited by conservative policies. For example, guns were supposed to crush us with women. The GOP experts said it was a toxic issue—women hated guns. The liberals certainly thought women hated guns and were afraid of guns and would vote like zombies for anyone saying he hated guns. We must not have known the same women.

When we talked guns to women, we emphasized that they needed the right to have weapons to protect themselves from rape and to protect their kids from whatever hideous fate the thugs liberals won't lock up would inflict. When liberals started babbling that guns are more dangerous to their owners—which is nonsense, but facts never stopped them—then we would demand that Democrats stop telling women what women need. We invented a catchphrase, "We can choose for ourselves!" and it just infuriated the liberals.

We pushed them to start passing laws and statutes that made the liberals squirm. We did that at every level, from city council to Senate.

The possibilities were endless. We were the ones who started pushing for laws that set the expectation that able-bodied Americans will support themselves. The American people loved it—at least the majority that worked to support itself—and it infuriated the liberals who had to block them and explain their votes later. This idea actually sowed the seeds for the Thirty-Second Amendment.

We pushed for restrictions on lobbying designed to keep politicians and their staffers from cashing in. That was really popular with voters, but the liberals hated it—it was a threat to their power base. Sure, some GOP hacks got squishy about it, but we pointed out that no liberal president like Obama or Hillary would ever sign these bills even if the Democrats let them pass Congress. The liberals became the ones stopping commonsense reforms, not us!

Oh, and we used the phrase "common sense" all the time. Liberals hated having to take positions against "common sense." Wherever we had control—county boards of supervisors, state assemblies, the House of Representatives—we would advise our people to pass bill after bill that embraced good, old-fashioned common sense—in the most covertly partisan manner possible.

We weren't bipartisan. We were about destroying our opponents, flat out. After all, our opponents were looking to destroy us. They even tried to outlaw us with the "campaign reform" laws under Hillary Clinton. It was sickening that you could actually be put in jail for advocating your views, but that was liberalism.

This was a fight to the death, and it was important that our people understand that and not pine for some bogus bipartisan fantasy world of the past. We needed to install the killer instinct into some of these people. The people who came in as candidates inspired by the Tea Party were okay. They wanted to draw political blood, and they understood that it was a death match with liberalism. The moderates, the squishes—well, they did not understand that the liberals would take their goo-goo, cloying nonsense about "good government" and turn it into liberalism.

We needed to teach them to say "No" to all manner of liberal nonsense. There could be no compromise with progressivism, just "No." I got furious at one whiny congressman who was bab-bling to me about compromising on something and I shouted, "Getting half a shit sandwich still means you're getting a shit sandwich!" It scared him into voting the right way. That and the fact that I told him I was going to go find a primary opponent for him if he didn't.

It was hard to get some of them to reject the shit sandwich. A lot of them were perfectly happy holding office in a permanent minority. When you expect to lose all the time, it's a lot lower stress than when you expect to have to fight for your principles every day.

We had to turn around a lot of losses. Even after Obama was reelected and started to melt down with Obamacare and the budget and Iran, we found ourselves still having to fight to just keep the House. The bipartisan, good governance idiots shoved through the immigration amnesty bill. We didn't take the Senate, which was ours for the taking, and nearly lost the House. What were they thinking doing something the conservative base made absolutely clear was a deal breaker? Our people were disgusted—and rightly so—and so they stayed home. They only came back when we primaried the bastards who sold us out in 2016.

We didn't take any chances with the good, solid conservative politicians in Congress. We buttressed the vulnerable members, which required the grassroots outreach that the overpaid GOP consultants hated but we excelled at. Once we cleared out the squishes, we were then able to go after vulnerable Democrats ruthlessly. The Obamacare fiasco had created a lot of vulnerable Democrats, and it was the gift that kept on giving as new prob-lems arose year after year.

Most Democrats came from districts much more conserva-tive than Washington, DC, is, and that bipolar activity made

61

them vulnerable even before parroting the president's lies turned them into liars too. We started early, recruited solid candidates—preferably ones that were bright enough not to spout off about rape—and took the fight to the enemy. The 2018 election wins that mirrored 2010 built on years of hard work and started setting the stage for eventual victory.

3

REACHING OUT

"We Were Selling What Young People Loved and Progressives Hated—Freedom"

There was always a huge tension on the right between two factions. The more cautious, moderate faction became the establishment and, to the constitutional conservatives, it was distinguished by its acceptance of the premises—and the perks—of power. In the eyes of the rebels, the establishment conservatives went on tedious Sunday morning talk shows like *Meet the Press*, circulated through Georgetown cocktail parties, and plotted with progressives in the guise of "bipartisanship." In response, the establishment was barely able to hide its contempt for the rebels and failed to see that the "sit down, shut up and vote for whoever we pick for you" attitude was fueling the fire.

The constitutional conservatives were the only place people with any libertarian ideas could go, as the establishment rejected them outright. That led to a critical mass of libertarian impulses among the constitutional conservatives, who rapidly discovered that if they wanted to succeed they needed to avoid picking fights with their new allies over the small issues. Libertarianism presented an ideology that made papering over these very real differences intellectually coherent. It also opened up the ability to attract young, tech-savvy voters alienated by progressivism's economic failure and tyrannical impulses.

Then there were the immigrants. The immigration issue was enormous in the first two decades of the century, with progressives partnering with establishment conservatives to pass a "reform" that essentially opened the floodgates to low-skill immigrants who were expected to vote reliably Democratic—while nearly destroying the Republican Party. After conservatives took over the reins of power in the mid-2020s, they made what was widely seen as one of their biggest errors, repealing the "pathway to citizenship" that millions were already on. The immigrant issue had always been difficult for conservatives, but while many immigrants viewed the insurgency as a threat to themselves, others embraced it.

And, of course, Hillary Clinton's abandonment of Israel in its time of need made many formerly liberal Jews reconsider the constitutional conservatives.

The libertarian and minority outreach effort was a success, but the immigration outreach failed. The consequences of each attempt still reverberate today—and will continue to do so in the future.

■ ■ ■

Tamara Hayes Smith (Professor/Activist)

One thing the establishment never understood was the libertarian impulse that surged through the constitutional conservative movement. GOP establishment figures were as much a part of the "big government" mindset as their liberal comrades—they could not conceive of any other paradigm. This led them, in many cases, to feel more at home with liberals than with members of their own party. And that mindset also kept away a substantial number of libertarians who were repelled by the GOP's intermittent embrace of big government solutions. It took years to undo the damage George Bush's "compassionate conservatism," which was really just a relabeled progressive republicanism, caused with libertarians.

Tony "Gator" McCoy (Chief Advisor to President Carrie Marlowe)

Gator is on his fourth beer and it's not even noon. The sun is up and the Florida humidity is getting to me. I finally accept a Coors and let the campaign legend ramble on.

There was already one big outside group that was largely on our side, or at least gettable. The problem was that with all the conflict over our relatively few areas of disagreement, it was hard to see it. It was the libertarians. These folks not only shared many of our core values but also—if they were actual libertarians, and some weren't—had huge issues with the soulless slide to fascism with the progressive status quo.

"If" was the operative word because many people who called themselves "libertarian" had the "lib" syllable down really well, but the appropriate suffix was "-eral" rather than "-ertarian."

If you thought you were a libertarian and you spent all of your time worrying about TV preachers banning masturbation and zero time about free enterprise getting strangled, you were not a libertarian. You were a liberal, and you probably needed to get a girlfriend.

65

Then there were the crazy libertarians, who looked sane and could hold up a conversation until they slipped in their worries about "chemtrails" and then moved on to telling you that their Ford wouldn't start and it was probably the fault of the neo-cons.

"Neo-cons" meant "Jews," and those kinds of libertarians were against them. So my feeling was that they could kiss our collective ass. I wasn't wasting any time on them.

The libertarians we wanted were the ones who pretty much wanted to be left alone, which was admirable. That was most of them. Wanting to be left alone is totally antithetical to everything liberalism is about, so we had that in common. We could build on that foundation.

We couldn't fool ourselves into thinking that we had everything in common. Libertarians tended to think—and some still think—that the only legitimate defense policy for the United States is locking ourselves inside our local Alamos and waiting. They got all squishy over drone strikes during the terrorist wars, which I never understood—how can anyone have been against raining fiery death on jihadists? We cons, well, we loved that shit.

Also, they tended to dig pot. Lots of pot. And they liked to talk about hemp for some reason. I don't know how many times I got buttonholed by some stoner telling me how George Washington raised hemp. Great! Now vote Republican! The best argument against marijuana decriminalization I ever heard was that if it passed, they'd never shut up about their stupid weed.

Some of us had a controversial idea—that we put off our fights with them and focus on beating Hillary and her statist pals. Certainly, there were some libertarians that thought, "Wow, conservatives are generally against abortion—I can't work with them on anything," which was as counterproductive as us thinking,

"Wow, libertarians are generally against restrictions on abortion—I can't work with them on anything." We have had plenty of time to fight with them after we ran those Marxists out of DC in the 2020s. But we agreed on probably 90 percent of things. What did Reagan say about that? That made us 90 percent allies, not 10 percent enemies? He said something like that.

Now, the road to getting support from the libertarian libertarians overlapped with the road to getting the young and hip people in our corner. I knew it could be done. The smarter ones among the young and the hip started to realize pretty quickly that liberalism was a giant scam where they do the working and the sweating for the government hacks and unemployables who made up the Democrat base. Hell, Obamacare was based on the idea of healthy young people being forced to buy too much health insurance for too much money so old people who had already had their chance to make money got theirs cheaper. Obamacare was a huge opening for us. It drove them away from liberalism, but not directly to us. We had to earn their support. And we did. We were selling what young people loved and progressives hated—freedom.

We started talking about other generational scams. For instance, Social Security was also basically a system where people like them gave money they barely had to older people who didn't save. They just got tired of being suckers, and that was our opportunity.

Now some of these young people's wackier libertarian beliefs initially rubbed us the wrong way, but they also deserved some examination. Carrie Marlowe was, of course, very interested in legal reform designed to repeal laws that did nothing but criminalize people for essentially doing little or nothing wrong. Sometimes it was for drugs; sometimes it was just to protect businesses. The Dems had played along with their donors, and the independent agencies were busy criminalizing things like reprogramming your cell phones. Seriously, you could go to jail for doing something to your own property.

We got to argue that we had no business running a criminal justice system for the benefit of giant tech conglomerates. We won a lot of young, libertarian people by pushing for the reform of copyright laws that criminalized normal folks to protect big entertainment companies. Young, libertarian-leaning folks loved it. The Dems, being the party of the status quo, couldn't do it. We cons could, and did.

Why not build networks with the enemy's voters while punishing the jerks who support the liberal establishment with their cash? It was a win-win!

There was also drug law reform, which would bring in a lot of young people, libertarians, and especially minorities who were seeing a shocking number of their young men locked up. This was a tough bridge for cons to cross—hell, watery-eyed stoners lazing about on their moms' couches halfheartedly watching reruns of *Star Trek: Fifth Generation* is everything we hate. But again, this was where conservative principles about small and limited government started crossing streams with our electoral self-interest.

Did you ever see *Ghostbusters*? Not the remake but the original from back in the 1980s? Do you remember the power of crossing the streams? They had these lasers and if you crossed the streams it was really bad, except at the end of the movie they did that to destroy the giant marshmallow man. Anyway, we crossed the streams with drug law reform. I guess liberalism was the giant marshmallow man. And we sure fried it too.

Our policies were not enough. We needed to go to those folks and make the conservative case, not just once for the cameras but continuously. So we did. Colleges, minority neighborhoods, places no Republican bothered to go consistently. And for years we got nowhere, but we kept going back.

When television networks were still big and I was working in DC for a big GOP consulting company, I would ask, "Hey, who is the go-to constitutional conservative guest on Univision, on BET, even on the damn Syfy network?" They'd book a conservative—we just needed to stop sending uptight dinguses who reinforced the reasons why these folks disliked conservatives in the first place. I mean, they sent one guy to the Azteca network for a news show and he spoke Spanish like a gringo and wore a freaking bow tie. *¡Muy estupido!*

We started to use technology to cultivate potential converts and we targeted them with information and social media. Obama was using a data-mining system for turnout early on, and Hillary's effort was even bigger. Supposedly they could tell you what some random guy's magazine subscriptions were and figure out how he was likely to vote. We got that sophisticated too.

I found out some interesting data. Conservative males? *National Review* and *American Rifleman*. Liberal males? *Mother Jones* and *Modern Bride*.

Juggs? A red-blooded conservative male.

Barely Legal? Probably a liberal male, and usually a senator from New Jersey.

National Enquirer? Definitely a Ron Paul fan. Remember Rand's dad, Ron? I shouldn't talk bad about him. As nuts as he was, he saw that the Hillary monster was the real enemy, and he really helped by lending his credibility to us to approach libertarians in '16 and '20 while he was still healthy enough to do it. I always said that Ron was crazy, not stupid.

Anyway, we needed that kind of information and more to

identify and focus on likely converts to conservatism. Instead of giving hack consultants a zillion bucks for some pie in the sky, top-down failure, we got some rich dudes to fund a bunch of entrepreneurial conservative tech guys to make this happen. Our donors didn't get a meet and greet with any senators out of it, but they actually contributed to something more than the mortgage on the consultant's Aspen summer home.

Regardless, the effect of these high-tech efforts was huge. The payoff was shaving just a few points off the Democratic share in some of their solid voting blocs, but that was enough. Libs always just slid into office with a tiny margin. Our effort helped destroy their solid voting blocs, which was awesome.

Back in the dark days, when Obama had been reelected and everyone was talking about doom and gloom, they asked, "Can it be done?" I said, "Why not?" Voting blocs are never permanent—the Democrat lock on the black vote was hitting the half-century mark. Before that, a lot of blacks had been Republican.

Eventually folks were going to wake up and realize that they had spent the last decade treading water in a sea of collectivist failure. We just needed to be ready to welcome them. Race and ethnicity correlated with being against us rather than for us due to decades of Democrat agitation and propaganda. We worked to turn that around.

Back then it took real bravery to be both a minority and a conservative. You had to have guts. The social pressure could be overwhelming. So that's where we needed to begin. We needed to be welcoming to nontraditional conservatives. And how do you be welcoming? Step one: don't be a jerk. Fortunately, cons tend to be pretty tolerant. They're real live and let live types, so most were good to go.

But decades of propaganda had totally wrecked our image

in some communities. We are still dealing with the fallout today. Back then, we needed to reach out and prove ourselves because, fair or not, we had nearly zero credibility in many minority communities. Yet we had one advantage the liberals didn't—conservative policies didn't cause the problems in the minority community, and some minorities, especially young ones, saw that.

We reached out to people who we did not see as allies. We accepted 50 percent friends, folks we could count on just half the time—a vast improvement over 100 percent enemies. We invested in the technology that allowed us to make these inroads, to identify those who might be approachable, and to make those approaches.

And sometimes we had to make tough compromises. As Florida's governor, Carrie announced that "the people of Florida have spoken" after the initiative vote to allow same-sex marriage. Our supporters were split on the issue, some for, some against, but there was a vote and it was perceived as fair, so after it happened we moved on to fighting the progs. We didn't ditch social issues. Some we won on, some we lost on, but the point is we didn't dwell on it. We made a point of what brought us together, not what could drive us apart.

Jack Archer (Democratic Strategist)

The GOP kept counterattacking, passing laws that made them look good but always cut into our Democratic constituencies. Like the drug stuff—they got to our left on drugs and all of a sudden we're hemorrhaging young people and minorities who couldn't stand mandatory sentencing.

I hated those conservative bastards.

71

Dagny Eames (Libertarian Activist)

Eames, who denies being named after the Ayn Rand character ("It's a family name"), understands how important an ally the libertarian community was. Initially suspicious of the constitutional conservatives, particularly of their perceived social conservatism, libertarians soon realized the deadly threat to liberty posed by the progressives—the NSA scandal shifted the entire paradigm. Constitutional conservatives, as a group, tended to avoid social issues, focusing on what united them. However, many constitutional conservatives were active in the pro-life and traditional marriage movements.

With the understanding that working together did not mean agreeing on every issue, the libertarians joined the fight. The campaign for federal decriminalization of marijuana—opposed by the Clinton administration but supported (generally) by constitutional conservatives who saw the massive assault on liberty posed by the drug war—led to huge losses for the Democrats in the 2022 midterm elections as a majority of young people found themselves voting Republican.

Two things initially kept me and many other libertarians out of the constitutional conservative movement. First, there was the Republican alliance with big, corporatist business, which we saw as undercutting true free enterprise. That changed pretty quickly as the constitutional conservatives started seeing how they were being played by rent-seekers. So that issue was relatively easy to deal with. What wasn't so easy was dealing with the social issues.

There were a lot of libertarians who were very concerned with what they saw as social conservatism running amok. They kind of went in two categories. There was one kind of libertarian that was pretty overwrought about it. They really thought that if the constitutional conservatives got into power, you would see things like bans on premarital sex, stoning for adultery, and detention camps for gays. Some of these people were crazy, some were stupid, and others were simply liberals who called themselves libertarians. It was hard to deal with these folks because they had already made up their minds—in their version of libertarianism, the most important things were these social issues and the rest of the liberty agenda simply didn't matter much to them.

They were never going to be convinced to fight the liberals, ever. The liberals could limit free speech, attack religion, expand government exponentially, and these libertarians would remain convinced that the biggest threat to liberty was the chance that constitutional conservatives might gain power and somehow outlaw blow jobs.

They marginalized themselves. By about 2022, they were the only ones left in the Libertarian Party since the rest of us libertarians had left because we knew we had to stop Clinton, and the only practical way to do it was an alliance with the constitutional conservatives. That meant the Republican Party. When the conservatives did retake power and then didn't ban sex and fun, as it were, then these people really had nothing left to offer to justify themselves as a movement. There's still a Libertarian Party out there. It's more of a name than anything else. The guy who runs it does it out of his apartment in Bangor, Maine. His name is Larry something—if I'm not mistaken, he ran for president last time and got about 12,000 votes out of 100 million or so cast.

But I don't want to seem like I am making light of the differences we had with social conservatives. Social issues were important to me, and we had real disagreements. Gay rights, gay marriage—these were important to me on liberty grounds, and people who felt like I did were definitely in the minority in the constitutional conservative movement. The drug war too. I was also pro-choice on abortion. But the social issues were not the only consideration to libertarians like me. They were just one part of the big picture. Our liberty was under attack.

What I and many other libertarians came to understand was that these issues were not front and center for the constitutional conservatives. That's not to say no one cared about them, but with all the other terrible things the liberals were doing to the country, as things got worse, these issues faded more and more into the background.

There was a real libertarian core in the Tea Party at the beginning, and that stayed true as the movement grew and matured. It was always very, very civil rights focused. Guns, for instance—it was hugely focused on gun rights, which most of us libertarians felt was vital.

When the NSA intercept news broke, they were very concerned with that. They understood the danger of government oppression because they were suffering from it. The Obama administration was using the Internal Revenue Service to harass and intimidate opposition groups on the right. As the Clinton administration attacked free speech rights, they were very pissed off, and that was a huge area of common ground.

In fact, we had so much in common that our disagreements, while real, simply weren't that important. Now, when we took power, there were some conflicts. We disagreed, had a vote, and moved forward in dismantling the Leviathan.

However, I think a lot of the issues resolved themselves. By the mid-twenties, gay marriage was generally accepted by pretty much everyone. It had been going on without any real consequences for 10 to 20 years by then, so it was a no-brainer to formalize it at the federal level.

The drug issue was interesting because it was the social conservatives who pushed letting up on it as a moral issue, citing the damage it was doing to families and communities. So there, we actually found ourselves standing with the people who were supposed to be our opponents.

The constitutional conservatives turned out not to be the people the media portrayed. They sure weren't prudes. Let me tell you, the constitutional conservatives were not about to ban sex. They liked sex—they are still the most fertile demographic group in the United States! And if you think they were some sort of antisex zealots in their private life, you should have been with me at some of the CPAC conferences in the 2010s!

Ted Jindal (Technology Consultant)

A second-generation American (his parents were immigrants from Mumbai), Ted Jindal was initially confused about where he fell on the political spectrum. But once he found his place, he saw that he and the establishment had much to learn about employing technology effectively.

I was a tech head, but I was very at home with the conservatives. I didn't start out really that conservative, but the more I saw of how the liberals had stacked the deck against young people and how real conservatives embraced creativity, I knew where I belonged. And they appreciated my skills.

I started working on ways to link conservatives using social media. The tough thing was that it was so decentralized that it was tough figuring out what resources could be used by the most folks. See, everyone was doing something different, so they needed different things. Some were running for office, others were activists on the outside, others were writing or making videos. The technology was the easy part—figuring out what was needed by a bunch of amateurs was hard.

Puff (Hemp Advocate and Activist)

Puff—no, not his birth name—is an enthusiastic advocate of living what he refers to as "a bong-focused lifestyle." The herb-friendly activist's face is famous from the "Like, Jail Would Harsh My Buzz" street art campaign for marijuana decriminalization, and in person he is exactly as one might expect.

I met him in his garden, surrounded by towering marijuana stalks, where he relaxed (after a bowl full of "tasty premium") and discussed how conservative support for decriminalization helped build bridges with communities not generally known for their openness to traditional conservative ideas.

I like smoking weed, and these guys didn't want to throw me in jail for it. That sold me. I figured if they were cool with what I was into, like getting high, then I was cool with their guns and getting government off their backs. So were my buddies.

They didn't have to like how I live my life, and I didn't have to like theirs. Live and let live, man. I could get into that. Want a bong hit? This stuff is killer—I sold the rest out at the store, but I have an eighth left if you want to fire up.

Tony "Gator" McCoy (Chief Advisor to President Carrie Marlowe)

We have left the relatively bug-free confines of Gator's porch and are walking through the woods, beers in hand. Gator ignores the buzzing insects—and, apparently, the effects of several brews, even as I slap and scratch at the swarm. Gator notices my predicament. "I could use DDT out here, but I'm too damn lazy to bother. You know, by lifting the stupid DDT ban, we saved probably a few hundred thousand lives in Africa using it on malaria mosquitos. Liberals love third worlders, but not enough to let them kill the bugs that are killing them." I push him on one of the least successful aspects of the insurgency, the immigration issue. He frowns.

Bar none, repealing the citizenship process for those already underway was the dumbest decision we made during the Marlowe presidency. We stopped millions of illegals from turning into freshly minted Democrat voters. But we also managed to turn immigrants and their families from kind of disliking us into wanting to string us up by our balls.

We still haven't fixed it. Yeah, it was a shitty law. Yeah, "immigration reform" was a scam and they passed it through fraud, but the damn illegals did what we told them to do and on the verge of citizenship we pulled out the rug. That's going to kick us in the ass for decades.

We fought against the amnesty law—we fought hard. They called it the "HOPE Act," but I'll be damned if I can remember what the letters H-O-P-E stood for. I think the "H" was for "Helping" or some damn thing.

Of course the liberals were all for it—they expected that it meant a ton of new voters for the Dems, and they were right. Our polls were all crystal clear. Most of the illegals turned

77

citizens would be voting Democrat pretty much forever. See, right there you would think that Republicans might oppose it, but you probably don't remember the old establishment Republicans we were stuck with back in the 2010s when Obama and Hillary were around.

What pissed us off was the people in our own party who just wouldn't look the facts in the face. Amnesty was a bill to create new Dem voters, straight up. But there were Republicans who supported it—a lot of them. I still don't get it.

Some were big business types who just wanted more cheap workers and more customers. Walmart was a huge behind-the-scenes backer. Others were these smug jerks who kept telling us how thought it was the "right thing to do." When some politician tells me something is the "right thing to do," it pegs my bullshit meter. You want to do the right thing? That all starts with beating the lib you're running against. Period.

Amnesty was political suicide for the GOP, but that didn't stop the establishment types. See, the old Republican establishment had this kind of suicide pact mentality where they felt honor bound to jump on a sword. Damn, the libs loved those mavericks—until, of course, the mavericks actually did something remotely conservative. Then they stopped being adorable mavericks and went back to being racist sexist homophobes who wanted to murder the homeless.

What really steamed us was how these squishes would try and act like we were some kind of racist haters whenever we brought up how having a few million people wander north into our country without permission and start taking government handouts bothered us. The American people like the rule of law, and illegals were, well, illegal. We were supposed to ignore that and act like we were in the wrong for caring?

Remember that one-term Cuban guy from Florida who everyone thought was going to be president? I actually helped out on his first campaign against this ex-Republican weirdo who became a Dem. Oh man, do I have stories about that guy. Anyway, that senator jumped on the amnesty bandwagon and just lied left and right to us. He told us it wasn't second, expanded amnesty and of course it was. He lost reelection mostly because we conservatives abandoned him, but when Hillary signed the amnesty bill he came back to DC. There are photos of him smiling behind her as she signed the bill. What a tool.

We hated that law, but the fact was that by the time we got into office a lot of people were using it to move towards citizenship. So, we had a choice about the facts on the ground. We could live with it and try and fix some of the problems, like how it didn't build a fence, or we could repeal it. The problem with that was a lot of people were in the pipeline already. The law was terrible, but they were obeying it.

We decided to tank it. Without a filibuster—thanks Harry Reid!—repealing it was easy, and that's what we did. But that left all these folks hanging—they'd started the process to become citizens and then we went and told them we'd changed our minds. Not surprising, they and their families were pretty pissed off at us.

Looking back, I think that after amnesty passed and they got invested in it, we should have switched strategies and fought for their votes. Instead, we now have this angry bunch of immigrant relatives who are citizens here that libs can use as a base to try and make a comeback down the road. They didn't move as far right as the rest of the country over the years, partly because we had trouble reaching them through Spanish media. Of course, we've deported a fair number and with the border wall up there's no more tidal wave coming north. Still, we kind of stepped in it with repealing amnesty. There were no good choices, and we chose the worst of them.

Rob Patel (President-Elect)

At the mention of immigration, the president-elect seems annoyed for the first time as he paces across the floor of his suite.

The whole "conservatives hate immigrants" thing always ticked me off. I mean, I'm part Indian, but not like Cherokee Indian! I'd have to hate my own family. And most of my family is Republican.

We have to understand some hard truths. First, America is the most conservative, which elsewhere would be liberal democratic, nation on Earth. We've gotten even more so over the last 20 years. Even the other English-speaking countries are to America's left on almost every issue. So, just about anyone coming here is to the left of the American mainstream. The immigrants from developed countries are shocked by what they see as the lack of basic welfare state institutions, and the ones from the third world are used to various degrees of socialism. Sure, a few of the countries are trying out American-style reforms and hope to copy our success, but it's a culture shock. So that immigrants usually start out on the left shouldn't surprise anyone.

This is particularly true about Mexico, where another part of my family is from. Mexico should be a rich nation—it's full of hard-working people and has great natural resources, but the fact is that the culture embraces a kind of socialist *caudillo* model where the government rules the people and not the other way around. A lot of Mexican and other Latin American immigrants get here and they bring the values of their home-lands with them.

And when it comes to the role of government in people's lives, those immigrants have a very different view than Americans. They think government should have a big role in people's lives, and we constitutional conservatives don't. It's a tough challenge for us.

Javier Salazar (Immigrant Worker)

Salazar earned his citizenship after enlisting in the United States Air Force as a drone maintenance crewman, but many of his family members had their processes cancelled by the Marlowe administration.

I was furious. People were counting on citizenship. They'd followed the law, even if they hadn't in actually coming here.

But that wasn't the only thing. I could never understand these conservatives. They seem to hate the government and want people left out on their own. That's something I don't believe in. I work hard, my family works hard, and we contribute. We aren't lazy, but sometimes we need help and that help isn't there from the government anymore. We used to have healthcare through the government and now I have to go find my own. I won't ever vote for one of them.

Jack Archer (Democratic Strategist)

The retired Democratic strategist smiles.

We own the Latino immigrant vote *forever*. I mean, they never had a chance at it in the first place. Even John McCain—remember him? His daughter has that awful talk show—anyway, he only got like 30 percent of the Hispanic vote and he was a liberal on the immigration issue. Boy, they sure took a bad situation and made it worse. Thanks, conservatives!

Ngo "Nate" Swazile (Immigrant Entrepreneur)

The legal Nigerian immigrant owns 20 cabs in New York City, something made possible by the deregulation of the industry over the last decade.

I will always be Republican. Always. Some say Republicans hate immigrants, but this is not so. They do not care. They leave us alone to make our own way. I do not need help and I do not need regulations that hurt my business. I just want to run my business.

I employ many people. They come from everywhere, and I tell them, "Today you drive a cab, but Allah willing someday you will have your own cabs if you work hard." I tell them, "You must vote for the Republican at all times because the Republican will leave you alone to work and the Democrat will not. The Democrat will take your money and give you nothing back."

Yitzhak Weitzman (Israeli Immigrant)

I met up with the noted novelist in a New York café, not far from his home in Manhattan. He was in downtown Tel Aviv on November 30, 2020, about two miles from ground zero. The left side of his face, the side facing the blast, still looks noticeably different. Blast burns are common in survivors—Weitzman calls them "the new camp tattoos." They are a mark of resilience in the survivors and a mark of shame for those who allowed the atrocity to occur.

After aiding in the rebuilding, Weitzman left Israel for the United States at age 33. He won several awards for *The Flash in the Sky*, his novel about the attack. Like many American Jews, both new and old, he found himself surprised to be drawn to the constitutional conservatives.

I was a socialist, for all intents and purposes. And I felt that we Israelis were largely in the wrong. I was very active in the peace movement there, very active. When Obama essentially allowed the Iranians to get the bomb, I thought it would pressure Israel to make concessions for peace. In retrospect it is hard to understand, but the things the Iranians said about burning the Jews off the face of the Earth and such didn't resonate. I chose not to believe them, as did Hillary Clinton obviously.

I was going to get breakfast when the bomb detonated. The air raid siren went off and I looked up, more puzzled than frightened—when was the last time an enemy plane or even one of Hezbollah's primitive rockets had broken through our air defenses? It did not occur to me—or, tragically, to the Mossad—that a pair of Russian officers would sell an advanced cruise missile to the mullahs.

There was a bright flash and then heat on my face. People ran and screamed. I looked off to the south. It exploded in the air on the outskirts of the city instead of over the government center where it was aimed—only the Iranians could miss a city with an A-bomb—and the fireball was rising.

I was stunned. I just stared and watched. I am lucky not to be blind. But what was even more shocking than the blast itself was what it did to me inside. In that blast, everything I had believed changed. I realized I had been a fool.

I was a peacenik one moment and then in the next I wanted

83

bloody vengeance. I just assumed that the IDF [*Israel Defense Forces*] would retaliate with its own A-bombs. But Clinton demanded we not do so and actually set the US Air Force against us. American stealth fighters shot down the planes carrying the retaliation strike to Teheran while they were over Saudi Arabia.

Clinton promised to make the Iranians pay, but even as our city burned and we were burying 30,000 of our people (ironically, many were Arab-Israelis, since it detonated over the predominately Arab Jaffa section of town), we watched the news showing the Iranians laughing and singing, celebrating in their streets. Untouched, unpunished.

Clinton promised retribution. She would land American forces and take their vital facilities on the Persian Gulf coast and then, somehow the Iranian people would throw off the mullahs and all would be well. It was magical thinking, and for me it was especially painful because it was the kind of magical thinking I had indulged in my whole life up to that time.

There was no revolution, of course. The mullahs were not about to let that happen. Clinton had hollowed out your military to such an extent that it would have been difficult to sustain the operation even if she had not placed politically connected incompetents in command instead of warriors who would tell her hard truths. What credibility America had not already lost when it acted to stop Israel's retaliation was gone as the invasion force retreated or surrendered.

I came to America near the middle of Clinton's second term, in 2022, and I was surprised to find it a sadder, weaker nation than Israel. In Israel, the attack had brought us together, and in some ways made us stronger as a nation. But I found that Clinton's America—which was supposed to be vibrant and rich and powerful and free—was none of those things. The economy was stagnant. There was no hope, just droning liberal propaganda about how the hard times and the government's mistakes were the fault of others—of anyone but the liberals in power.

I expected a free exchange of ideas, but people warned me not to speak publicly about the failings of the Clinton administration. "You'll get the IRS on you," they said. "They'll deport you. Keep quiet. Don't make trouble." This, in America!

I was never quiet when I was on the left and now, on the right, I was just as loud. I submitted an article to the *New York Post*, which printed it, to its great credit, even though it ran afoul of the noxious "Fairness Law" the liberals used to stifle dissent. It was called "Liberalism's Betrayal of the Jews," and it got a lot of attention. Unfortunately, *I* got a lot of attention too—they started trying to deport me, and I was fighting that in the courts until President Marlowe ended all the retaliatory administrative actions once she was inaugurated.

I argued that, as Jews, the constitutional conservatives were the only force in American politics we could put our trust in. The liberals, we had learned to our great sorrow, had no principles except the pursuit of power. If we Jews became inconvenient, we would be discarded—and we had been discarded.

But the constitutional conservatives believed in freedom and justice and not merely power—in fact, what I liked most about them was that so few seemed to want power. They seemed vaguely annoyed that the liberals had forced them to take time away from other endeavors to retake their country. And many of them were either Orthodox Jews or evangelical Christians—despite the leftist lies I had learned about these Gentiles as a young man, these religious Christians were our people's greatest friends on Earth.

I found that constitutional conservatives were not seeing the world through the same hyperpoliticized lens that the liberals

85

were. They had no political need to overlook the barbarism of Israel's enemies. They knew an enemy when they saw it, where liberals never could—or rather, because of their ideology, refused to do so.

And constitutional conservatives felt no need to interfere with the lives of the people. For liberals, the personal was the political, and they felt compelled to insert themselves in every aspect of human existence. It was liberal cities and states where you would see petty harassments and insults like attempts to ban circumcision. It would never occur to a constitutional conservative that this was any of his business. In fact, they saw these progressive attempts to interfere with our sacrament as repugnant.

I found many of the American Jews I met politically and culturally confused. The bombing finally drove some out from under the heel of liberalism, but others couldn't escape. They were too far in. It was too big a part of their identities. Most were secular, like me, and liberalism seemed to fill a void in them that religion would have in another age. Despite everything liberalism did to them, every failure and every betrayal, some simply could not reject it. But enough did that there is no longer a solid Democratic "Jewish vote" in American politics.

4

REGULAR PEOPLE

"I Was Just a Normal American Who Was Scared to Death"

The conservative insurgency was not fought by Washington insiders, though some played a part. Even if the people are sometimes led by a cadre, insurgencies are essentially of the people and by the people. These regular people activated and acted without centralized leadership, yet the synergy of their shared focus exponentially increased their power. But it was not only "ordinary" people or clichéd conservatives—liberalism and its appetite for total control of every aspect of life pushed non-conformists who would otherwise be leftists into the insurgency.

■ ■ ■

Sandy Crawford (Conservative Activist)

Underneath a portrait of a smiling Andrew Breitbart, Sandy Craw-
ford pauses for a moment to take a phone call. It's one of her grand-
children; she gives him some advice, then ends the call and returns
to our talk.

My kids are why I did it, why I got involved. You have to understand. I was frightened for them and for my country. A lot of
us were. Everything I had seen my parents work for was falling
apart. The country was being changed into something I didn't
recognize, and something that seemed to hate normal people like
me. I was just a normal American who was scared to death.

Obama came in promoting this "hope and change" crap. And
it was crap—it was simply a power grab for coastal liberal elitists. He was elected right after Wall Street almost collapsed, or at
least said it was about to collapse in order to get its bailout. The
national debt was staggering. Prices were increasing, and the
Democrats targeted us, the regular middle class folks, the only
folks who by no stretch of the imagination were responsible for
the crises he was claiming to be solving.

We Middle Americans did everything right. We worked hard,
played by the rules, as Bill Clinton used to say. But the liberals
hated us. You could tell.

The liberals saw us as the enemy. I think it was partly because
they were snobs—they hated our traditional values and looked
down on us as ignorant and unsophisticated, even though studies
showed that we were better educated. I think it was also partly
because hating us was useful politically—they could tell the takers
who voted Democrat that we were why they were failures. But I
also think there was another thing—we didn't *need* the liberals.

We could rule ourselves, without them, and they hated us for it. If the whole country were like us, self-sufficient and responsible, there'd be no need for liberals. That scared them, and they were right to be scared. That's what we changed the culture toward over the last 30 years, toward self-sufficiency and independence, and that's a big reason the liberals are locked out of power today.

Americans today don't need them.

Looking back, you can see how we were the perfect demographic for a mass movement like ours. Many of us had built our own careers and businesses, so we had skills. And Obama pushed exactly the wrong button with us, the red button that would activate us. He said the one thing that forced us off the sidelines.

He came in and told us—and I remember this vividly—that we "didn't build that." Right there, the liberals attacked the entire foundation of who we were. They were trying to delegitimize anything we said or did. They tried to steal away the moral value of our hard work, you see. Then we would be defenseless and submit. We would need them and their pack of liberal geniuses, just like every other demographic block. There'd be no one left who they didn't control.

It didn't work that way.

I was fuming, but I wasn't sure what to do. I heard about this Tea Party thing from the mainstream liberal media, and I just instinctively knew that if the liberal media hated it, it had to be good. I got involved. I had no political experience, but I went and saw Andrew Breitbart speak at a rally during a snowstorm in Indiana. He was a visionary. He understood our potential. He treated us like we had power, like we had a right to express our views and defend what we had built, and he urged us to exercise it.

I started listening to conservative talk radio. Rush Limbaugh, Mark Levin, Hugh Hewitt, and others—I was in Indy and listened to Greg Garrison a lot. That was crucial—it helped coordinate us and build morale. You could turn the radio on and you could hear people putting into words what we all were thinking. The Tea Party rallies did the same thing—I never thought so many other folks felt like I did. The media sure wasn't going to tell me.

I devoured conservative books. The Internet was crucial too. Facebook, Twitter, conservative websites—we just went around the media gatekeepers and built networks of contacts. You learned you weren't alone.

So I found myself in the movement. It wasn't like you signed up. It wasn't "community organized" by some cadre of George Soros–funded leftists—if you showed up and did stuff, you were in the movement. There was no barrier to becoming active. You just did stuff and you were part of it. We never really talked a lot about the goals or even about the ways that we conservatives, as a movement, could wage a peaceful insurgency. See, *you* aren't a movement—*you* were an individual and an American citizen doing what you felt you wanted to do to advance what you believed.

So, I asked myself, what do *I* do? How should *I* be a part of this fight?

Well, at first, I had no clue.

It didn't take me long to come up with some ideas, but the point was that neither me nor anyone else needed to get some kind of order from on high and then to go salute and carry out the mission. The great strength of our movement was that it was individual action—"decentralized" is how some people describe it. The fact that there was no rigid hierarchy or structure trying to manipulate all the levers of the movement was an advantage. It allowed for experimentation, and the most effective ideas rose to the top.

That made us more agile than the centrally planned left. Decentralization meant that *you* had to figure out what you could do best to contribute. Only you knew your strengths and weaknesses, your situation, your preferences, your resources, and your opportunities. Only you knew how you could best be a part of our cause.

Decentralization leveraged each individual's ability to act in the most effective way to achieve the maximum results for his efforts. See, when running a community organizing effort like the left did, you didn't have to be so targeted. You had a ton of resources, and the sheer bulk of the organization would allow you to overcome the inevitable skills/talents mismatches over the long haul. With the constitutional conservatives, we needed to fit the round peg in the round hole—we couldn't just pound any peg through any hole because our figurative hammer was so damn small. Instead of some organization organizing the pegs to the holes, we self-organized as individuals.

In other words, we weren't so big or overwhelming as a movement that we could afford to forgo the benefits of precisely matching individuals to our needs. So the way that conservatives did that matching is the same way the free market does it—decentralized self-selection. People picked jobs because they felt they would fit the need. So, not only did we maximize our talent pool but we reaffirmed our core principles.

People who knew how to write drifted toward writing. Web people drifted to web tasks. There were a lot of people who were really good at speaking, and they drifted toward radio. Guys would just start shows on the web and then—*voila*! They would land terrestrial radio shows!

This wasn't really surprising. Even if we could have organized ourselves some other way, we largely came out of the small business, entrepreneurial world. Many of us owned our own small businesses. We applied those same skills to the cultural/political fight.

All this is a really long way of explaining why I needed to figure out on my own how I could best contribute to the movement. But the key was that we needed people to contribute somehow—time, money, effort, whatever—if we were going to beat the liberal establishment. We needed real people. We couldn't hope to convert the populace without the help of people within the populace.

I found I was a good organizer. I had run a small crafts store for a while but closed it up when the kids came along. Yet even with the kids, I was a den mother and soccer coach and generally, well, a general! I knew how to get stuff done—I was always the one the PTA called to set up dances and such—so I used that skill to organize for the Tea Party in Indianapolis.

But I wasn't a fighter, at least not yet. And this was a fight.

The first step was to gird your loins for battle—this game was not for the weak or the faint of heart, and our progressive opponents got meaner and more obnoxious and even worse the closer we got to the moment they realized their crappy little ideology was heading out back to the Dumpster.

No one was asking us to stand up to a volley of British musket fire like the Minutemen, but we soon saw that we were going to be smeared, lied about, mischaracterized, intimidated, and threatened. I got audited for the first time the year I became chairwoman of my local Tea Party group. But if you couldn't take that hit, then we might as well have packed that whole freedom thing up, drunk the Kool-Aid, and started singing that "Mmmm, Mmmm, Barack Obama" song.

You remember that song? Schoolteachers, unionized of course, would make the kids sing it like in some third world dictatorship. It was a terrible time—it was like liberals were trying to create a cult of personality. That's the thing about liberals—they reject God, but it leaves an empty space they need to fill and they try to fill it with liberal icons. I personally think that liberalism is a symptom of emotional emptiness—it's like an ideology based on weird daddy issues.

Anyway, we realized that we were effective and that we mattered, especially after we kicked their tails in the 2010 midterms. But in 2012, we realized that we were it. There was no one else. The establishment Republicans certainly weren't going to fight this fight. It was just us.

If we didn't win, we were going to lose our country forever.

Remember my friend—really, he was thousands of peoples' friend—Andrew Breitbart? He saw it. He got it. Andrew's most important lesson to us may well have been that a decade before he died, he was just some regular guy, a normal American citizen who had had enough.

Just like me. Just like millions of us.

The issue was not whether you *could* be part of the fight. You could. The question was what could you *do*?

Most started at the individual level. You had to start somewhere, and many—even most—people are not really comfortable in the limelight. But you didn't have to be debating some androgynous lefty pundit from DC on MSNBC to be in the fight. Regular folks had a vital—I'd even say decisive—role to play.

As an individual, at the personal level, you could engage in

93

three main ways—by contributing, modeling, and interaction. Of course, no one used those labels at first—we just sort of naturally understood the basic concept. But when millions of us started to engage in these three ways, the results were earthshaking.

Contributing was just that: contributing your money and time to the cause. We had a lot of organizations that did a lot of great work. For example, FreedomWorks organized and trained activists, while the Pacific Legal Foundation pursued a "lawfare" strategy. The NRA defended our Second Amendment. They all needed dough. It was easy to write them a check!

Conservative candidates needed money, and they also needed volunteers. There was where we shined. We got in there and volunteered for the guys running against those hard left congressmen, or the soft right ones who would come home and tell us they had our collective back, then return to Washington and stick a knife in it.

How else could people contribute? Well, people talked a lot about moving into the media and entertainment spheres. If there was an outspoken conservative star—it was so rare back then that it's hard to believe today—we would go out of our way to see his movie or watch his show. If there was a film that seemed even remotely conservative, we would give it the benefit of the doubt and go see it.

Geez, I saw some terrible movies for the cause. But our viewership watered the seeds of conservative entertainment until it could take root in popular culture and get past liberal prejudices and gain an audience.

Support for conservative writers also created an audience that the mainstream publishing community could not afford to ignore. We knew that you couldn't fight in the battle of ideas if you don't even get to the battlefield.

Modeling was huge—huge. I don't mean modeling in the sense of attractive women marching about in lingerie, although conservative men were very open to this—there was a whole meme about how conservative women were more attractive than liberal women. I mean modeling in terms of living your life in a conservative manner as a model for others to emulate. The media could and did disrespect conservatives all it wanted, but actually living a conservative life, displaying solid values and demonstrating how they lead to success and happiness, was a powerful rebuke to the tacky chaos liberals excused in the personal lives of their constituents. When you modeled what happens when you live conservative values, people had to take notice.

Sure, much of the establishment hated us for it—but they really hated themselves. We got used to that kind of projection. Many of them lived in chaos and despised us for demonstrating that life didn't have to be an endless series of government hand-outs, broken families, and failure.

Modeling worked both ways—liberals who modeled bad behavior (especially Hollywood stars and rappers) caused enormous social damage. But when a liberal inadvertently modeled conservative behavior, it was useful. As much as Barack Obama's policies were awful, his model of an evidently happy marriage with two beautiful children probably did more good for our country than anything else he'd done, including giving the SEALs the reluctant thumbs-up to pop Bin Laden.

We needed to be that model in our own individual social circles. And we demanded that conservative leaders do a better job of modeling too. The last thing we needed were more "conservatives" caught up in skeevy perversions—we were less concerned about their own personal failings than about how liberals could

95

twist their scummy antics to tar all of us and, more importantly, the values we actually embraced.

My feeling was, and many conservatives shared it even at the beginning, that if you're gay, come out and be gay. We could deal with that—there were a lot of gay constitutional conservatives. Just don't be dragged out of the closet because some vice cop drags you out of a bus station toilet stall.

Oh, and we encouraged people not to be a married traditional-marriage advocate and then get caught banging someone they weren't married to. Hypocrisy rolled off liberals' backs, since at their core they don't believe in anything except their own power. Because we said we believe in principles, we got held to them, and hypocrisy gravely hurt our cause.

Now, interaction was just that—it meant interaction targeted to your own social circle to try and convert the undecided middle to our cause. Facebook, Twitter, Tumblr, Instagram . . . these were our first online tools. Our goal as individuals was not to change the world, but just our little piece of it. This is where we could correct misinformation about conservatives and our ideas—who didn't have some granola-crunching lefty jerk get on their Facebook page and wail about how we need to ban "automatic weapons with high-caliber clips"?

Somebody had to respond, and that was us as individuals operating in our own little individual network of friends, relatives, coworkers, and acquaintances. We learned to correct misinformation, clearly, concisely, and competently. The mainstream media sure as hell wasn't going to get the truth out there. We were each the truth squad for our own social circles. We stopped allowing progressive memes and deceptions go unchallenged in our individual worlds.

Whether you linked to a great article or re-tweeted one, or whether you wrote something short about your own experience, individual Americans were each powerful advocates for the conservative cause because they had personal credibility within their social circles. People *knew* them. Those droning Marxists in the media only had sway if there was no countering voice, and individual conservatives—someone their friends knew and trusted and respected—were that counter. We outsourced the job of mainstream media rapid response to ourselves!

Then there was personal involvement. We started going to city council meetings, to Republican Party meetings, to PTA meetings, and we made sure that the only people talking weren't liberals and squishes. There was this creepy liberal movie star that liberals just idolized no one remembers anymore except for two things. First, he married his adoptive daughter, and second, he said that 90 percent of success is just showing up. He was right about the second thing, but a skeeve for the first.

We conservatives started showing up.

We made sure we served on juries. Now we were politically aware, and we enforced the law while forcing the government to do its job. Unjust prosecution over guns or free speech or even raw milk? We voted to acquit! Nonsense, frivolous lawsuit? We gave the bum nothing. We reformed the out-of-control legal system by doing our job.

And we needed to vote, and make sure our friends and neighbors (at least the ones who weren't liberal) voted too! Constitutional conservatives provided the people power for the Republican Party even as the establishment heaped contempt on us. That's how we ended up taking it over. We were the ones who knocked on doors, made phone calls, and organized like-minded patriots. We *were* the Republican Party.

Hey, it wasn't going to happen if we didn't make it happen. So, damn it, we made it happen.

There were so many ideas, options, possibilities—but the individual conservative was in the best position to decide what he or she could do. They would come into the movement, look around, see what was happening, and determine where they could make the biggest difference.

There was no end to the potential ways to contribute for a conservative individual. Remember, Andrew Breitbart was just some guy. He *chose* to be more. He worked at it. He learned to speak in public and to use the new media to get his views out there. Why couldn't you start a conservative blog? Or write for an established one? They loved to break new writers—loved it! Why couldn't you host an Internet radio show and podcast? There were so many ways to contribute.

The opportunities were unlimited.

Sometimes we got ahead of ourselves. If you were a regular citizen, you might figure, "Why not run for Congress?" Believe me, congressmen aren't anything special. They sure aren't necessarily geniuses—I worked on a few campaigns in the 2010s and 2020s and believe me, Capitol Hill has never been an arsenal of intellectual firepower. It wasn't a meritocracy. If you were conservative, and you mastered walking upright and could form a coherent sentence, you could run for Congress as a conservative and still be a better candidate than most of the establishment politicians. But that was still problematic.

We soon figured out that the first run for elected office for a conservative should not be for Congress unless the candidate happened to have a couple million bucks to toss into his campaign war chest. And if he had a couple million bucks lying around, he could have probably done more good with targeted contributions to conservative organizations than by running for the House.

What about the local school board? The local water district? How about the city council? Newcomers had a much stronger chance at these levels, and we never underestimated the importance of these positions, particularly as we worked to devolve power back to the governing bodies closest (and most responsive) to the people. You could make a substantive difference right away by advancing constitutional conservative principles right there in your own community. And by taking those offices, we were also working for the future.

We needed a farm team. We needed future leaders. And those jobs were the farm team. That's where the next generation of conservative leaders, the ones coming up who just got elected with President-Elect Patel, started learning the craft of politics. That's where they got training, built networks, made contacts and, critically, make mistakes. In 2012, we lost two Senate seats because the geniuses running screwed up. They were right on the issues, and much better than their opponents, but they were stupid and they made mistakes.

If you are going to disqualify yourself from future office because you are too damn stupid not to refuse to offer your moronic opinions about rape, I think it's safe to say we'd all have preferred that you did it a campaign for a place on the 23rd Iowa Sewer and Utilities District than when running for the seat that determined who controls the Senate.

And let's not forget the Republican Party offices, the chairmen and committeemen and others who actually had a lot to do both locally and at the state level. I remember one of them telling me how he was outnumbered 85% Democrat to 15% Republican in his district and next telling me how he had been the party chair in that district for the last 15 years. It was time for some new blood. We were the transfusion.

Very few people thought about these intra-party jobs, which made them vulnerable. They were just kind of handed to the same people over and over because they kept showing up over and over at the selection meetings. And the sleepy timeservers who usually held them were often squishes who wanted people like us to shut-up, fall in line, volunteer and write checks, no questions asked. No one really ever challenged them, so they just continued on down the same path of mediocrity and failure, more concerned with retaining their titles and perks than kicking liberal ass.

In case you misunderstood my point so far, I'm here to kick liberal ass.

Their complacency made them vulnerable to focused, dedicated challengers who could assemble a voting bloc of constitutional conservatives that would sweep the sparsely-attended elections for these posts. Look at the Ron Paul folks back in the first decade of the century—every election they organized and then came in and pick off a few unsuspecting local GOP structures. And those folks had it even harder than us—I mean, have you ever tried to organize libertarians?

Whether your turf was your own social circle or whether you aimed for political office or public activism, if you wanted to take this country back from the collectivists who wanted to turn it into a warmer Sweden, then you needed to act. In the end, it all came down to you as an individual. Otherwise, forget it—there was no one else, no outside cavalry squadron that was riding in to save the day. It was all on us as individuals. All of it.

DANN
AUS

xxxxxxx0542

7/18/2022

Item: ï¿½0010082660605 ((book)

Each of us had to figure out what we could do, and then go do it.

Sister Margaret Feeney (Nun/Religious Rights Activist)

I meet the feisty Catholic sister at St. Bart's Hall, the food kitchen for the down and out that she has run in Seattle for decades. She pitches in with dishes after the lunch meal, joining the recipients who "pay" for their food by helping to clean up afterward. She is a tiny woman, much smaller than she seemed on television twenty years ago when she was one of the most public faces of the struggle against the religious bigotry of the left, but she still seems young even though she is in her seventies.

It was the Obama and Hillary Clinton administrations' vicious regulatory assaults on religious freedom that turned her from a quiet monastic into a media-savvy rebel. Putting away her cleaning rag and grabbing herself and her guest cups of hot coffee, she sits at one of the long benches in the hall and begins.

I was not interested in politics. All I wanted to do was express God's love through helping people. I feel that's why I was called to the Church and to the sisterhood in the first place. As things got worse in the country, I tried to escape it by diving deeper into the work, but I realized that there was no way to escape. It was escape-proof by design.

The progressive goal was to eliminate any spaces that they did not control or dominate. It was not enough that the Church tried to stay out of active politics—and it did try, hoping it would be left alone. But it could never be left alone. The progressives could not allow any alternative power centers to exist. As meek and humble as we tried to be, they could never tolerate us. They

101

had to destroy us, and when I saw that I realized that being meek and humble was not going to do the job.

They had to break us, to make us betray our own faith by accepting their secular premises. We had to be humiliated and forced to act contrary to our values. That was why forcing us to contribute to abortion funding was so important to them. By making us collaborate, they would break us.

It was part and parcel of what they did throughout society. They would use discrimination laws to persecute businesses whose owners had a moral objection to gay marriage and didn't want to participate by baking cakes or taking photos. There were plenty of bakers and photographers out there who would, but that wasn't the point. The point was to make people bow down before them.

They used insurance to persecute us. They wanted us to pay for abortion practices, including the so-called "morning after" pills. Well, that was absolutely against our deepest values. This made it even more important to the liberals to bend us to their will. They said we were denying women health care. Of course, if you couldn't afford to buy your own birth control, perhaps you ought not to have been having sex.

They went out of their way to rub our nose in the changes they were forcing on us. It was so ugly, so hateful and vindictive. They could have easily found ways to protect our consciences, but that would have been contrary to their real agenda. They wanted us on our knees before their false god: government. Well, this lady kneels to no one but the Lord!

Colonel Jeremy Denton, US Army (Ret.)
(Insurgency Expert)

The colonel looks more like a senior professor, albeit a very fit one. He's very patient with me, a civilian, as he explains to me—slowly— how insurgency differs from what we generally think of as warfare. It is not a battle of similar forces, like two armies with tanks and artillery clashing on a battlefield, but rather of two very different forces both in form and goal.

An insurgency is about people. It is focused on the people. You need the people to buy in, and because insurgency is decentralized, they have to act independently. But no group of people is homogenous—you have tribes or clans or other groups, many of whom hate each other, but to beat the establishment they have to come together somehow. So, you need the people—regular people—involved, and you need them to work with others they might not normally associate with.

This is a key point about insurgency—unlike traditional warfare, it doesn't focus on enemy forces or on terrain. It focuses on the populace. Insurgency theory is a very detailed subject, but simply understand that to the insurgent, *the hearts and minds of the population is not the only part of the battlespace, but it's the most important part.*

This is key. The conservative insurgency sought to win not just terrain—think of that in terms of institutions and social spaces like academia, the media, and political offices—or to defeat enemy forces like specific politicians and leftist activists. It sought to win over the people to constitutional conservatism.

Our end state was not just a government run by constitutional conservatives, nor even a media, entertainment industry, and

103

academia where conservatives could compete, but an American citizenry that once again wholeheartedly embraced constitutional conservatism. That generally meant reestablishing the cultural norm of personal responsibility as opposed to entitlement, and reinforcing the understanding that individual autonomy takes precedence over government power.

If we didn't win over the people to those concepts, then our victories would just be transitory. The next election could see our progress wiped out. Instead of having the Thirty-Second Amendment, we'd still be fighting about government handouts. But because we won the people over, because we changed minds about not just what government should do but what people were expected to do to support themselves, the argument about personal responsibility is over.

In the end, the conservative insurgency was about truly fundamental change—or, perhaps more accurately, fundamental change *back*.

Without that change, sometimes we could have a solid conservative president, sometimes not. That's not good enough. We *always* want a constitutional conservative president, so we wanted the mainstream political spectrum to stop on the left end well before we got to liberalism, much less socialism.

That was the real goal of our movement, even if no one put it into those words at the beginning. But that's no surprise that we didn't articulate out goals precisely. Most insurgencies don't start off with a well-thought-out plan. Most start out like ours—a bunch of people angry at the status quo who start acting independently.

The conservative insurgency centered on a few key principles. First was decentralization. We weren't one single, big organization or even a cohesive movement. That was a lucky break. It would have given the other side a target. Look at what happened to the Tea Party, a model of effective decentralization initially. The Tea Party was subjected to the full force of progressive hate, from the media, academia, Hollywood, and politicians. The Obama and Clinton administrations even used the Internal Revenue Service, the Federal Election Commission, and other government agencies to attack it. Remember how they persecuted any organization with "Tea Party" in the name? And soon there was no more Tea Party, yet there were still millions of us who were part of the movement it represented and were still active even if fewer people wore the label.

Our opponents were fighting a phantom—there was no *there* there, which is why all their hate and anger and effort came to nothing. There was no "Tea Party" to crush. We didn't give them anything to destroy, so they couldn't destroy it.

Next was the principle of individual effort. A decentralized organization means there is no one telling individuals where to go and what to do. In the Army, the bureaucracy decides your military occupational specialty and off you go. The needs of the whole organization matter, not your desires or talents. If the Army needs you in the infantry, you go in the infantry even if you always dreamed of being in military intelligence.

But in the conservative movement, you could do what you wanted, contributing in your own way, supporting conservatism as you followed your own desires. Artists made art. Writers wrote. Businesspeople did business. But they all did it with an eye toward expanding constitutional conservatism.

Let's take one industry as an example, the movie industry. By the 2010s, liberals went into the movie industry to meet girls or guys and make money, and if they could promote liberalism too, that was fine. Liberal ideology was no longer a motivating force. It was burned out, more of a default setting than anything else.

But conservatives started going into the movie industry to meet girls or guys and make money, but also to consciously promote conservatism. And the same with reporters and professors and government officials and so on. We were a force of individual insurgents, all operating at our maximum effectiveness, independently, whose collective efforts led to victory over time.

We needed a political consciousness. Insurgents must have an ideology or they are useless. They just won't undergo the hardships they need to over the extended time periods they must endure them if they aren't committed to something more than just their petty personal interests. Ten men who believe in something are the match of a hundred who are just drawing a paycheck. We believed, but the failure of Obama and later Hillary meant that the liberals no longer did. It was all a lie to them; liberals repeated the words but they didn't believe them. They just wanted to maintain their power and position. This was a huge advantage to us.

We promoted and reinforced our constitutional conservative beliefs and values, and they kept us going all the way to victory. Remember, we always had to keep in mind that thanks to the progressive threat, everything we did—from having a family to working a job to simply living conservative values—had become a political act.

No, we didn't ask for the personal to become political, but it did and it still is. Maybe now that we have banished the pathology of progressivism from our body politic we can go back to normal someday. I hope so.

We had to learn to attack where the progressives were most vulnerable. An insurgent does not waste his efforts putting his strength against the counterinsurgent's strength. He finds the enemy's weakness and masses his power against that weakness so to maximize the effect.

Think about a guerrilla band in the jungle, perhaps of company size, about 100 troops. Do they attack a company of the counterinsurgents? No, they hit a platoon of say 20 troops, making sure that in that one small fight the correlation of forces favors them.

And they don't just hit enemy forces. They swoop in and mix with the people when the counterinsurgents are gone. They find the unguarded bridge the counterinsurgents need and blow it up. They use whatever they have to make it difficult for the counterinsurgent. We needed to hit progressives where they were weak. And, as we found, they were weak all over. That's what happens to a force that realizes that its ideology is based on lies.

We needed to fight everywhere and in every way. This was not just a political fight. We couldn't win without winning elections, but we couldn't win by *only* winning elections. We needed to take the fight to every one of progressivism's redoubts and sanctuaries, the places where they thought they were safe and had let their guard down.

Academia, the media, the entertainment industry—the liberals thought that they owned them all. But technology was on the way that made their grip on the legacy means of distribution that used to mean power (the campuses, the newspapers, the movie studios, the networks) less and less relevant. We had a golden opportunity to move into their sanctuaries and clear them out, and we took it.

While it didn't seem like it at the time, as Obama and Hillary were tearing apart the country, in reality, time was on our side: the insurgency was not going to be over quickly. The progressives

107

really started moving in the 1960s (or even before) and only then, a half-century later, were they truly on the cusp of realizing their nightmarish vision. They underwent a long march through our institutions and reached the summits, but there's one thing they didn't count on. All that marching left them exhausted, spiritually and ideologically.

If they ever believed that their scheme was about anything more than raw power, that illusion has long since been discarded. Liberalism was a spent force as a political philosophy. The only reason it could still fight us was that it had sheer weight on us. It was ripe for defeat, and it didn't take us half a century to make our own march back through the institutions.

After all, they had to impose a twisted, alien ideology upon a free people. We were selling freedom to a people born hungry for it. And they could try to hide and excuse the manifest failures of their ideology for a while, but not forever—the truth was all around us, like "Going Out of Business" signs and health insurance cancellation notices. The truth was going to win out—we learned, though, that it would take some time, that we were in it for the long haul. But every day, we got stronger, and every day, they got weaker.

As with any insurgency, we insurgents advanced in phases. David Galula's famous book *Counterinsurgency Warfare* discusses the classic communist insurgency model. Phase one is to create a party; that is, an ideological infrastructure. Phase two is to form a united front, which means enlisting allies. Phase three is guerrilla warfare, actual combat, but not as equals with the counterinsurgent force. Phase four is movement warfare, fighting the counterinsurgents as equals. Phase five is the annihilation campaign, where the insurgent is now stronger and destroys the counterinsurgent in detail.

This is not a perfect fit for how we did it in our conservative insurgency, but it's pretty close. Through the Tea Party's embrace of the Constitution and the existing conservative intellectual structure of institutions and publications, we completed phase one and created our ideological infrastructure. We didn't have a Communist Party promoting rigid orthodoxy, but constitutional conservatism did have a coherent set of values and principles and institutions to discuss, explain, and promote.

To the extent the Republican Party tried to fit the bill, we had to take it over first. There was a lot of heartburn about that, but revolutions are always full of infighting between factions with marginal differences. Think of the GOP establishment as the Mensheviks, except wimpier and whinier and even less competent. But it was a structure, and taking it over was smarter than trying to build a third party from scratch like some people advocated.

The united front envisioned in phase two was important. We needed allies, even ones who weren't a hundred percent in line with our views but for whom progressivism was likewise a nightmare. Libertarians were the first to join, but there were other groups that soon did as well, like college students. Many Jewish Americans left the Democratic Party and found their way to us after Tel Aviv.

The key was to have allies, and sometimes we had to soft-pedal or even modify peripheral policy preferences to enlist others in our cause. If we could destroy progressivism for the price of letting Bob Marley–loving potheads fire up their bongs without getting arrested, we were getting a bargain.

Phase three was active conflict, where we used every one of our limited assets in the most effective manner possible across the entire spectrum of society to challenge the left. Over time, as we began to prevail and become stronger (and as progressivism

109

became weaker), we could meet them on equal terms. Conservatism, not milquetoast GOP moderation, became the sole opposition.

We knew we were in phase four when a constitutional conservative ran for president and won in 2024.

We are still in phase five, finishing the job, figuratively rooting progressivism out of its hiding places under rocks and in the dark corners of society. Our goal has been and needs to continue to be to annihilate its credibility and its false claim to morality so completely that it can never again rise to threaten our freedom.

The devil was always in the details, but still, the idea, writ large, was simple. Constitutional conservatism won by insurgency, by outwitting, out-organizing, and outlasting progressivism. It was the lean, committed guerrilla against the sluggish, exhausted conscript. And it couldn't lose.

Carla Quinn (Network Expert/Consultant)

Carla Quinn's company assembles and analyzes information for customers ranging from the Republican Party to Proctor & Gamble. Though the CEO of the multimillion dollar business, she still likes to keep her hand in what she still thinks of as the "fun part of the job" — analyzing how networks of different individuals organize themselves within society.

I started out as an intelligence officer in Iraq during the war. That's where I became fascinated by human networking. So, I was a new lieutenant out of the Fort Huachuca military intelligence school and all of a sudden I'm at a headquarters in Baghdad trying to figure out the Iraqi insurgency. Nobody had a clue—there were all these different groups and we didn't understand how their interests fit together. That meant we had no way to go beyond reaction and into offensive disruption. So I dived into trying to understand how insurgent networks worked. I started to see the insurgency not as a monolithic structure but a collection of decentralized actors, each with certain interests that would lead them to cooperate with other insurgents, sit out, or even oppose the insurgency.

I finished my hitch, went home, and started to work for an insurance company. The Tea Party movement is what made me politically involved—I was from Texas and freedom is in my blood. I found I was good at helping build networks of activists. I saw that various groups had differing interests, and that the conservative movement as a whole was failing to properly focus on shared interests and deemphasize disruptive ones. I also saw groups we had ignored—libertarians were key.

Plus, and this was very important, we started finding cracks in the liberal networks, cracks we could exploit to siphon off their supporters. We hacked their activist networks by picking the right people to appeal to the right groups on the right issues at the right time. Like Jewish Americans—obviously the A-bombing was a huge issue and it gave us a chance to reach out to people alienated by Clinton's botching of the crisis.

One big success story? Black Americans. Obama took something like 95 percent of black American's votes in 2012. It was practically unanimous. We got Carrie Marlowe 32 percent in 2024. That was huge. How? By working to build coalitions—sometimes one-issue, working coalitions—with unexpected groups. Business groups, church groups. We worked hard to identify any subgroup we could possibly connect with, even on just a few issues. Then we got the information out there through social media and personal contacts. It took a while for the GOP to listen to us, but eventually, when everything else failed, they did.

Jerome Timms (Republican Congressman)

Timms used to be something exceptional—a black Republican from the Massachusetts district that covers some of the toughest parts of South Boston.

My mom was going to be in jail for 20 years, no parole, because her boyfriend hid a duffel bag with a pound of rock cocaine in her basement. She wasn't a saint, but I don't think she even knew it was there. I remember the police hauling her away. I was seven and I was crying. So were my little brothers and sister. The conservatives got her out, and that's why I am a black Republican.

And I'm not the only one. I know the damage drugs did in my community. But I also saw the damage the drug war did, and without any real improvement. I can see how it affects my community today, but it is orders of magnitude better now.

And it wasn't the liberal Democrats we were supposed to vote for who made it better. It was those crazy conservatives who were supposed to hate us. Why am I a Republican? Because I respect the law, but I also fear it. That's an understanding liberals don't have, but black Americans and conservative Americans certainly do.

My family had been Democrats for generations. But President Marlowe signed off on school choice and I ended up at a magnet school and then at Harvard and Harvard Law on a scholarship for high-scoring poor kids. Yeah, poor—my problem was being poor, not being black.

Brad Fields (Insurance Salesman)

We are talking in Brad's office, where he oversees the dozens of workers his insurance agency employs. With Clemson football memorabilia and pictures of his family on the walls, he seems the opposite of a cunning insurgent.

I was getting more and more fed up with things and I was trying to figure out what I could do. My town gave me the answer—it decided to put out a ballot measure to raise the sales tax to pay for some ridiculous new building for the mayor and his cronies. So I got involved in the opposition. I started meeting people and making calls, writing letters to the editor. I started knocking on doors. It was a low-turnout election, but we were motivated and we beat it. I realized that we had real power, but only if we used it.

The local GOP structure was old and kind of inbred—a bunch of rich people playing at politics. I was young and pissed off, so I got in touch with the folks who had helped beat the county sales tax increase (which the local GOP hacks had supported!) and I ran for a committee seat and won. You would have thought I had farted in church with the looks they gave me when I took my seat at the first meeting.

Becky O'Hara (Education Advocate)

Becky O'Hara graciously gave me a few minutes as she packed up her office. Fortunately, there was not much to be boxed up—she had come into her job with the idea of shutting the organization down. Within a few days, she would leave, her mission accomplished. But for the moment, she returned to a time almost 28 years before, when she was just a typical suburban American mom.

113

In 2013, I got tired of my kids' schoolteachers and their creepy progressive indoctrination. They would be taking kids and making them write about how wonderful Obama was and asking them about who their parents voted for. Well, my kids naturally said "Mitt Romney" and the teachers gave them hell. Of course, the school's test scores were dropping, but they didn't care about *that*. It was unbelievable.

I had never been active before, but something had to be done and I decided I'd do it. I knew most of the parents at the school and I started talking to them, then Facebooking about what was happening in the district.

Then I had a meeting at my house. There were five of us, but we decided we'd all go out and bring at least two more folks to the next one. There were 20 people at the second meeting—I ran out of coffee and cookies! We used the web to link ourselves together, and I took some ideas from the FreedomWorks website about how to deal with local government agencies like the school board.

We decided to show up at a routine school board meeting—suddenly about 100 ticked-off parents walked in and I thought the board members were going to faint. Parent after parent just lambasted them. Finally, the chairwoman looks at us and, in a really condescending voice, says, "Well, we certainly appreciate your input, but we have *real* work to do now." I looked at her and it just sort of popped out of my mouth—"Oh yeah? Well I'm running for your seat!"

She laughed at me then, but she wasn't laughing when I won.

Lieutenant Jim Gallegos (Iranian War Vet)

Lieutenant Gallegos walks with a limp, one of a number of physical reminders of his time as a prisoner of war outside Teheran after the failed retaliation following the Iranian nuclear attack on Israel on November 30, 2020. Wounded severely during the initial amphibious assault to seize various strategic sites along the coast, the young Marine was abandoned in the chaos of the withdrawal President Clinton ordered after it became clear that the expected popular uprising was not going to take place. "We were supposed to be greeted with flowers," Gallegos recalls bitterly.

None of them in the Clinton administration had ever served in uniform. We military people were aliens to them. They didn't understand us, or trust us, or listen to us. The Joint Chiefs told the president that the force was hollowed out. I guess they didn't understand what that meant. They saw the military as a great place to take money from to give it to people who didn't feel like working. That cost a lot of people a helluva lot—lives, their health, years in Iranian dungeons.

But that didn't matter to the liberals. They turned on us and blamed us for not making up for a flawed plan, weak leadership, and inadequate resources.

I missed out on some of the most critical years of the insurgency being stuck overseas. But when I was released thanks to President Marlowe—she didn't take shit from the mullahs—I left the Corps and went home. New Jersey is deep blue and the state rep for our hometown was as liberal as they came. I ran against him and took it to him.

During a debate, he started talking about "liberalism means this" and "liberalism means that" and I got pissed. I took off

115

my shirt and showed the scars from the war and said, "See these scars on me? That's liberalism. The scars on our country? That's liberalism." That video went viral and I won the election. I served three terms and then turned the seat over to another constitutional conservative.

Flamenco (Performance Artist)

In 2041, the toast of Manhattan is edgy performance artist Flamenco. Pierced, tattooed, and of indeterminate gender ("I don't really believe in gender, but if you do, cool"), Flamenco gets noticed with often outlandish and bizarre installations that combine painting, dance, holography, and music. I was able to get a few minutes of the artist's time before a performance later that evening.

I've always been a conservative. I grew up in a liberal family. They were *really* liberal and so smug. All the liberals I knew wanted to do was tell me what to do. Go to this doctor. Don't drink a soda that big. No smoking! I hated it!

The liberals never talked to me about freedom. Never once. Liberals were always about controlling me! At college, I would get shit from the liberal professors when I said what I thought if it didn't fit in their ideological box. And the rules! Liberals love their rules—for them it's all about control. I once tried to do a performance that involved a little campfire in the college quad and five cops showed up. One Tasered me! And they gave me an air pollution ticket!

You know who never gave me grief? The conservatives. Oh, a lot of them weren't into what I was doing, but not one ever thought it was his or her right to shut me up. They never told me what to do. It was liberals who told me I couldn't smoke or speak up or whatever!

I kept hearing how conservatives were going to have me arrested for having sex. That never happened. It was all bullshit.

5

LAWFARE

"It Was Hand-to-Hand Combat in the Courts"

I am not a lawyer—like most Americans, what I know about the court system largely comes from videos and e-books. While most citizens don't understand the mechanics of litigation, we Americans still tend to see the courts as a venue where right and wrong battle it out. It's very binary—there is Atticus Finch, and then there are the bad guys.

The conservative insurgents knew this. They exploited the courts ruthlessly, especially in the early years when they literally had no other forum where they had to be treated equally and where their arguments could not simply be dismissed out of hand. It was a very special kind of cultural warfare. They called it "lawfare," and without it the entire movement might have collapsed.

■ ■ ■

Roberta Klein (Conservative Activist/Attorney)

The receptionist asks me to wait because the woman I am there to see is running behind schedule. I get the impression that's not unusual. The law firm of Parnell, Farrell, Moskowitz & Klein occupies the thirtieth through thirty-fifth floors of a sleek new office building in downtown Dallas, the nation's emerging business center. Its client list is a who's who of major corporations and wealthy individuals. After 15 minutes, Roberta Klein herself comes out and introduces herself with a handshake. She is short, even in heels, and immaculately dressed. "I'm glad you came personally," she says. "I'm old school. I hate video conferences."

Her corner office opens up on a view of the city so spectacular that I simply stop and stare for a moment. She smiles. Her walls are lined with photos, all signed, of the major movers and shakers of constitutional conservatism, past and present. Prominently displayed behind her massive maple desk is one showing her with President-elect Patel, both of them holding Mossberg 12 gauge shotguns, smiling at a skeet range.

The note reads, "Roberta, we could not have gotten here without you! Best, Rob."

She motions for me to sit in one of the reddish leather chairs arrayed before her desk, and begins . . .

They called me "traitor." Literally. And I would ask them, "Traitor to what?" I never got a straight answer, but I think it came down to me betraying my class.

I was a Yale Law grad and I was rejecting the unspoken assumptions of what a Yale Law grad was supposed to believe in and fight for. It was the school that produced Hillary Clinton, and here I was, frustrating her and her minions. I was trained and groomed to march along with my classmates into a progressive future and I was rejecting that. Hence, I was a traitor.

I used to say that I was not rich enough to be liberal. I made it into Stanford on a scholarship. My dad was a schoolteacher and my mom didn't work outside the house. I was bookish, but I had three big brothers who wrestled, so I could either be feisty or get pummeled. I chose to be feisty. I did very well on my SATs—that was the old college aptitude test—and got into the Farm, did well as an undergrad, and went on to Yale Law on another scholarship. I liked law because I figured I could use my brains and my feistiness!

I thought I was liberal. The first time I voted I voted for Obama. I didn't make that mistake again! You see, I actually believed in the Constitution. I thought the Bill of Rights was an amazing statement of personal freedom, and I thought that was what a liberal was supposed to believe.

But at Stanford, and especially at Yale, I saw the reality. Sure, they paid lip service to concepts like free speech, freedom of religion, due process, and so forth, but the second any of them came in conflict with some progressive prerogative, that was it. The rights went out the door when they stopped being useful to the cause.

But to me, those rights weren't just a pose. They weren't disposable.

I graduated, clerked for a federal judge, and then went off to a big law firm where I was one of a dozen new associates working 80-hour weeks. I was on track to be a partner, and focused almost entirely on business litigation. But I was required to do some pro bono work of my own choosing—the firm was very keen on looking like it was all about public service even as it billed out lawyers at $600 an hour.

Other associates were choosing to represent death row convicts, welfare recipients, detained terrorists, or artists mad because Uncle Sam was refusing to fund them covering themselves with milk chocolate to protest patriarchy. But me? I chose to help a Tea Party group that had been pretty effective in upstate New York, then suddenly found itself under all sorts of investigations by different New York state agencies. It seemed almost [*Klein stage-gasps for effect*] coordinated, as if liberal bureaucrats were targeting the group and its members for daring to effectively petition the government for the redress of grievances.

It never occurred to me this might be a problem for the firm—I mean, it was clearly government officials violating the rights of some little guys. I figured out how to get past some procedural hurdles and sued the individuals in federal court. Then all hell broke loose.

I got a call to come up to the partners' conference room. I had never been up on the top floor before. There were a dozen senior partners there, bigwigs who mingled with mayors and senators and CEOs and who would never even acknowledge me in the elevator, and now they were all looking at me.

They were not smiling.

They didn't ask me to sit. One of the name partners, who I later found out was a huge campaign contribution bundler for liberal politicians, pointed a bony finger and said to me, "Ms. Klein, what the *hell* were you *thinking* with this Rochester Tea Party lawsuit of yours?"

He said the words "Tea Party" like he was discussing an STD.

I was taken aback, but I am a litigator and like I said, I am feisty, so I guess I just forgot to be intimidated. "I was *thinking* that the government shouldn't harass Americans citizens because of their politics."

Oh, he was steamed. "This is not a lawsuit this firm wishes to be associated with. You will dismiss it immediately."

"No, I will do no such thing," I said. "The Rochester Tea Party is a client of this firm, and we owe it a duty to see the case through until it releases us."

I guess no one had told any of them "no" in a couple of decades, because they seemed too shocked to react. But I was not done. "And I do not understand your objection to representing a group of decent, hardworking people who just want to exercise their rights as Americans. I mean, are you saying that they somehow have less moral standing than the gentleman we represent pro bono who shot up that nursery school? Or that airplane bomber at Guantanamo Bay?"

Apparently, the answer was "yes."

They fired me, and they convinced a Bill Clinton–appointed judge to let them withdraw from the Rochester Tea Party case.

I did not have anything better to do, so I took the case on my own—via the Law Offices of Roberta Klein, which consisted of my apartment in Brooklyn and a post office box for getting mail since this was before we did everything electronically. I went to work on winning the case.

Here is the little-known secret about litigation. The trial and the jury and all the trappings you see on videos—that is only a part of the game. Yes, it is important, but as *theater*. Nothing that ever happens in a courtroom should be a surprise. You are not there to find out new things (at least, you are not intending to—sometimes it happens). You are there to make a presentation, to put on a performance, and hope that your audience— and our audience was, in ascending order of importance, the judge, the jury, and the American people—gets the message you are communicating.

123

We sought to communicate a simple message—your government is doing something very wrong, and you, as an American, must put a stop to it.

The real detective work comes in discovery. That is the phase where you gather evidence. There, unlike at trial, you *should* be surprised all the time, because if you are not finding out new and devastating information, you are not digging deep enough.

You sometimes see videos where the lawyers talk about "fishing expeditions." Well, discovery *is* a fishing expedition—and it is supposed to be one. There are very, very few limits on what you can delve into. Discovery is remarkably intrusive, but that was to our advantage. Our clients were small groups, like the Rochester Tea Party, and individuals. They did not have that much stuff to look through. But the government? It always has *a lot* of records and documents that might be relevant.

Discovery includes some very powerful tools. There are document requests. We would send out a list of categories of documents, like, "Provide all documents related to communications within your agency regarding, referring to, or discussing the Rochester Tea Party." Then the bad guys would have to go through all their documents and give us everything that was responsive. We would send hundreds of requests, and they would ship us back truckloads of documents. Yes, often it was on hardcopy paper back then, and they kept a record of *everything*. They would usually even print out the e-mails. It is a lot easier today with everything done electronically, but their convenience was the least of our concerns.

You can send interrogatories too. Those are written questions. One might be, "Identify each individual in your organization who undertook, participated in, or recommended any administrative action regarding the Rochester Tea Party." Then we would depose the people who were identified in response—question them under oath and in front of a court reporter—and start figuring out who coordinated the conspiracy against our client.

We would also send requests for admissions. If they admitted a request, they were bound to it. One might read, "Admit that a decision to assess an administrative penalty against the Rochester Tea Party based upon its conservative beliefs would constitute a violation of the civil rights of the Rochester Tea Party." I would hope they would deny that—and they usually would, using some tortured interpretation of the text of the request—so that I could get up in front of the jury and tell them that these bureaucrats and their agencies had denied under oath that targeting political opponents was a civil rights violation. That would set the tone for trial nicely.

Was I concerned with them lying? Heavens, no. They *always* lied. But they could not help their bureaucratic nature. The proof was always there in the documents, recorded somewhere. I spent many an all-nighter pouring over boxes of government documents until I stumbled on the smoking gun I could flash up on the monitor for the jurors to catch the bureaucrats in a lie and thereby win the case.

Rochester Tea Party v. Jemima Rudolph, et al., was the first of many cases. Rudolph was the head of the state agency going after my client. Soon, I started hiring associates, other young constitutional conservatives (because by then I had figured out what I really was politically) who were eager to fight.

There had always been a few conservative or liberty-based legal groups who would sue when the government overstepped, but we were part of a wave that took it to a whole new level. It really kicked in with the suits involving Obamacare and its

125

effect on religious and personal liberty. The progressives had nothing but contempt for people who did not agree with them, particularly religious people. They tried to use Obamacare to figuratively shove their opponents' faces in the dirt by, for example, forcing believers to subsidize abortion-related insurance. My whole goal was to survive in the case long enough to get in front of a jury, because then we would win even if we lost.

We started calling it "conservative lawfare," and it drove the progressives nuts. What made them so vulnerable was not only the dubious legal grounds of their actions but their manifest pettiness and unfairness. You see, lawfare—as progressives themselves used to understand—was not just about winning on the merits of a particular lawsuit. It was *theater*—it highlighted and put in front of the public these government actions in a way that could not be swept under the rug. You go to court, and unless you dismiss the case following a settlement, the court has to rule one way or the other. Something has to happen.

Most Americans are generally fair-minded, and they saw how essentially unfair many of these government actions were. And when the progressives doubled down—which they always did—they looked awful. It was not always a matter of winning or losing the case itself. We lost a lot of cases because Obama and Clinton had years to pack the courts with progressive judges, and many are still on the bench making mischief today even though impeaching those three Supreme Court justices during the second Marlowe administration sent a pretty clear message.

But what really mattered, what really helped the movement, was showing the injustice of progressivism. Lawfare let us do

that.

Colonel Jeremy Denton, US Army (Ret.)
(Insurgency Expert)

The colonel is particularly animated, pausing only to sip his black coffee as he focuses on the subject he spent his life studying—how to defeat an enemy.

Fighting a war is actually pretty simple in concept. Execution—that's where it gets complicated, but the concept itself is really, really simple. You never want to fight fair. You want to always—*always*—have the advantage. Most battles are won or lost long before someone fires the first shot. It's all about setting the stage for the battle, maneuvering yourself and your forces into the most advantageous position while simultaneously maneuvering your enemy into the least advantageous position.

We call that "shaping the battlefield." You look for where and when *you* have the edge, and then you make the enemy fight you there and then. That's especially important for insurgents. Our conservative lawyers understood that instinctively.

Dan Stringer (Billionaire CEO/Activist)

The notorious tycoon has just finished a tennis match. He is a fierce competitor and is clearly pleased that he won the match. His Ukrainian tennis coach hands him a fruit drink and a towel. He stands while he talks, leaning on the net.

I threw money at lawyers because we could *win* in court. We wanted to get the government and the progressives in court because that took away all their advantages. I was a big proponent

127

of lawfare right from the beginning because I saw that was where we could draw blood.

I funded a lot of lawyers. There was a glut of them, and I could get them cheap, so I found some talented ones and created a public interest law firm. I took the write-off—we were a nonpolitical civil rights organization under the law—and my lawyers raised unholy hell with the liberals, suing every government agency and liberal institution for everything they could think of. It was great. No case was too big or too small. The government was constantly having to get up and publicly defend its nonsense. Win or lose, we won. And what made them maddest was we stole that screenshot right out of their playbook.

I used to say that conservatives had to harness the power of lawyers for good instead of evil. The left had been using the courts for generations to chip away at our Constitution; we needed to use it to rebuild our rights and our freedoms. And, along the way, to give the progressives fits.

I learned that lawfare was not suited just to federal government issues; in fact, states often provided us an even more effective venue for litigation. I didn't realize it before, but my lawyers showed me how the state constitutions are just packed full of civil rights that dwarf what's in the United States Constitution. Moreover, with many states in conservative hands, we had the chance to do what the left was so good at and pass laws that empowered conservative activists to seek conservative change in the courts.

What were some good targets? Schools were great ones. There was nothing better than a lawsuit over the petty fascism of some principal who thought she was Stalin reborn. We had one who refused to have kids say the Pledge of Allegiance. Just flat-out refused. Well, many states have laws requiring the Pledge, but hers didn't. No problem for my lawyers! We cobbled together some half-assed civil rights claim and filed. Discrimination laws are awesome!

Now, some of the lawyers didn't get what we were doing. "Wait," sputtered one of them, who soon found work in the workers compensation law field. "This sounds legally tenuous. What about standing? What about, well, evidence?"

Silly lawyer. This was *lawfare*.

We knew we weren't necessarily trying to plead and prove a legally meritorious claim. This wasn't about winning some money. It was about defeating our opponents in public, about humiliating and demoralizing them while getting our own side energized. We filed that lawsuit because Principal Pinko wouldn't let Junior say the Pledge and that kid was on *Hannity* the very next day. The key element wasn't the legal brief. It was the press release. This was guerrilla theater.

We exposed the principal as some sort of liberal wacko and the superintendent started getting calls from parents—which he knew as "voters"—about why one of his administrators was dissing Old Glory. He picked up the phone and pretty soon the principal was chastened and the school day began starting again with the kids with their hands on their hearts pledging allegiance. I had a camera crew go out there and film it.

By the way, we didn't even bother to serve the lawsuit. We just cashed the settlement check and my legal team's next case had some seed funding.

It was a virtuous circle.

Most fair-minded Americans were appalled when we showed

them the kind of bigotry that, say, an evangelical Christian would have to endure at the hands of government bureaucrats or the big, liberal-leaning companies. Pretty soon, after burning their hands on the stove enough, the word got out—knock off the prejudice against these folks. We loved to get settlements that forced liberal government appointees or Democrat-funding CEOs to have to endure sensitivity training designed to cleanse them of their atheist-normative, urbano-centric biases. They became terrified of us.

That's how we covertly enlisted government agencies and private employers to help defeat the kind of bigotry that marginalized conservatives in society. We let *them* do the work of battling the bigotry against us. It wasn't just a few conservatives complaining about being treated like crap. Instead, we created a whole army of fussy human resources professionals rooting out discrimination against our people, spurred on by the desire to avoid any more lawsuits from conservative victims.

We made it expensive and inconvenient to hate us publicly. And after that, we focused on other key rights and freedoms—including ones that weren't really set out in the text of the Constitution. The right not to have your public school kid indoctrinated, the right not to have to pay taxes to support freeloaders, the right to concealed carry of firearms. The liberals had spent decades finding useful things between the lines in the Constitution; now it was our turn. As one of my lawyers said, we made those penumbras emanate!

Michael Ambarian (Supreme Court Justice)

I barely recognize the justice when I walk into the Alexandria hamburger joint where he suggested we meet. He's hunched over a view screen, working on what turns out to be his latest e-book, a biography of Antonin Scalia. His casual dress and calm demeanor belie his reputation as the most ferocious inquisitor on the High Court since his hero, Justice Scalia, retired in 2025 at age 89 a week after the inauguration of Carrie Marlowe. A half-empty pint of Guinness Stout rests on the table beside him. He notices me and motions for me to join him.

"What are ya drinking?" he asks.

I make it a point not to hire my clerks from the Ivy League schools. They used to produce nearly all of the law clerks for the entire federal system, and that kind of incest—oh dear, my critics will certainly jump on *that* slip—was very, very harmful to the health of the judiciary. You ended up with this kind of inbred groupthink that was inevitably progressive. I wouldn't have a problem with one strain of thought or another generally dominating the judiciary, except that progressivism happens to stand in precise opposition to the most basic premises of our constitutional system.

But more than that, I like my clerks with a bit of seasoning. *Life* seasons you, not seven years at some eastern college mingling with people who are exactly like you in an environment that is not only artificial but prides itself on its artificiality. I have to say that one of the best things to happen in the last few decades is the collapse of academia as it was in the beginning of the century.

I was seasoned nicely, I think, as a young lawyer. I have to admit that sometimes I miss my days as an activist attorney fighting for social change through the law. [*The justice smiles at his appropriation of that progressive cliché, and takes another drink of his stout.*]

We were always working, always fighting. Every day the Obama administration would try something, some executive order that had no basis in law, or employ some practice designed to make an end run around the Constitution, and we'd go right at them.

It was hand-to-hand combat in the courts. We were in federal court all day, and then in the office until midnight. Good times. See, conservatives had used the law before—the *Heller* decision on guns was a good example—but mostly as a *shield*, trying to undo damage. The feds would try to impose some mandate or restriction that violated the First Amendment—they *hated* the First Amendment, because it created an obstacle to their dominance—and conservatives would react. But you don't win by reacting!

So we took a page from the left, and we started using the law as a sword, not just a shield. We used it to force change in liberal bastions, but on our terms.

At first, we had to use the laws as they were. Later, as we started gaining political power, we could use new laws designed to facilitate our various campaigns. This was especially true at the state level—we'd work with conservative legislatures to pass laws like the ones expressly requiring faculty "religious diversity" and then use them against government agencies that discriminated against Christians and observant Jews. They *hated* that too.

We didn't have those at first, though, so we had to use existing law in new and creative ways. What was great is that we used their own rationales against them. One of my favorite examples comes from our litigation against various universities over their hiring practices. Our goal was to help break the liberal lock on higher education using the courts, since their love of diversity stopped when one suggested that diversity of political thought might be appropriate too.

We found some rejected faculty candidates—we made sure they all had outstanding academic records, of course—and sued for "discrimination" based upon a "disparate impact" theory. We were basically saying that the lack of conservatives on a faculty was *per se* evidence of prejudice against conservatives. We had seen this in race and gender suits in other contexts, so we applied it to *our* context. It's a very useful argument. You can't really fight it—if you have 35 professors and 35 of them donated to Hillary Clinton, it's pretty tough to argue you've grasped the Holy Grail of political diversity.

Now, I hate disparate impact analyses, and I think their application is facially unconstitutional. There are simply too many other factors at play to simply count beans and come to a verdict. And I unhesitatingly used disparate impact theories (and others I felt constitutionally suspect) mercilessly to defeat the progressives.

It's not hypocrisy, though I've certainly heard that term misused enough in describing how my record as an attorney supposedly contradicts my record as a jurist. Hypocrisy exists when one acts in contravention of his views. My view of the law, as an individual as opposed to as an attorney, was utterly irrelevant. An attorney must, as every state bar's regulations require, assert the interests of the client and advocate for the client using every available legal tool. The adjective for this representation that seems to reoccur often in the state codes is "zealously"—an attorney must "zealously" represent the interests of the client.

So, whether I personally thought it was a good legal theory, or bad legal theory, or an indifferent legal theory, I was obligated to assert it if it was to my client's advantage to do so. So, I was not even remotely a hypocrite for thinking "disparate impact" and other liberal concepts were constitutionally suspect while using them to batter my opponents with them.

Of course, the progressives got clever. They would argue that political beliefs were not protected under discrimination law—basically, that "conservatives" were not a protected class. We would later get many states to pass laws expressly remedying that, but sometimes this stopped us. So we shifted—we started amending our lawsuits so that the discrimination was not merely on the basis of political views but on religion as well. We'd allege that the faculty candidate was rejected also because he was a devout Christian or an observant Jew. This had, as Kissinger might say, the added benefit of being true. Then we'd hit them with a disparate impact analysis argument on *that* basis. Later, we got laws specifically creating these new protected classes.

The response was hilarious. Suddenly, the faculty would be filled with these deeply religious, devoutly spiritual academics who couldn't *possibly* discriminate against a fellow believer. So, I would take these depositions of these freshly minted theologians and ask tough questions like, "What church do you attend?" and "When did you last attend it?" and, my favorite, "So what's the minister's name?"

Even though it was pricey—and early on we operated on a shoestring budget—I always tried to videotape those depositions because their reactions were just priceless.

I remember one guy—I think he was a gender studies professor—telling me how he loved evangelical Christians, how he respected them, and how he was spiritual himself. I just nodded as he droned on, and when he was finished I reached into my bag to get my social media research out. It seems he was so proud of his achievement that he had to post on Facebook (remember Facebook?) his elevation to chair of something called the Organization of Academic Atheists. His entry contained several references to Jesus as a "zombie messiah," which he thought was very clever, and he insisted on spelling "Christian" as "Xtian."

We had a settlement within a week. I think we received a dozen slots on the faculty for conservatives as part of the deal. Settlements like those were conservatives' foot in the door, our beachhead onto those hostile shores.

Oh, that professor had to attend "religious sensitivity" training to ensure he could get along with his new academic coworkers. It was glorious.

We worked with friendly legislators very closely to shape the laws to support our legal campaigns. For example, we made sure that the laws provided that prevailing plaintiffs in cases like ours were awarded their attorney's fees. Remember, as my old law partner used to say—in fact, he had a sign hanging in his office to that effect—"It *is* about the money." While we sought injunctive relief—court orders for the other side to do or not do something—money really makes the world go 'round in litigation as in everything else.

Our clients needed money for damages, the bad guys needed to pay money so they would have a disincentive to reoffend, and we needed money to fund our campaign. The one-way fee shifting laws we worked to pass were huge for us. Progressives loved them in regular discrimination and consumer cases because they put pressure on the defendant to settle while the plaintiff had almost no disincentive to sue, since win or lose he wasn't paying the other side's fees. They did not enjoy contending with fees provisions when we asserted them.

In contrast, we loved our new laws. We could force change in anticonservative sectors of society and make progressive institutions pay for it!

We didn't always win, especially at first. We lost a lot. I mean, sometimes it seemed like we'd *never* win a case, but in reality we were winning big time where it mattered in the larger scheme of things. Our legal campaign was not about just getting verdicts— it was about showing the public what was happening in their country. We wanted to get on the news showing our carefully selected plaintiffs going up against a noxious, liberal government and private institutions. And we did, always in conservative media, often in the mainstream.

It was messaging. And what was key was that big donors started getting that the payoff from one of our successful cases was exponentially greater than the value received for all the cash they used to squander on mainstream Republican consultants. Once things started changing and we started winning, our legal campaigns started tearing up the welfare state. We crippled Obamacare well before Congress killed it dead.

It was a fun time. [*He smiles and chugs the rest of his Guinness.*]

Darcy Mizuhara McCullough (Former Missouri Governor)

The former governor fusses over her granddaughter as she recalls her turbulent tenure as a red state governor during some of the toughest years of the insurgency. Now 72 years old, she still displays the energy she brought to her office when it came to fighting the liberal federal government.

We were very aggressive in passing laws to address health care as a state concern, rather than implementing Obamacare. The Obamacare Supreme Court decision upheld the individual mandate as a tax, but Justice Roberts left a huge door open with his Commerce Clause holdings. We targeted the implementing regulations. And there were a lot of targets!

The federal government hated what we were doing in the state to reform social programs, not because it wasn't effective but because it was. They sued us to stop our reforms, and we sued right back.

We played hardball. The feds sued us and we fought. I must have doubled the size of the attorney general's office. All we did was sue the feds and fight them when they sued us. We didn't always win, but we made it so the bureaucrats started to try to avoid messing with us because they knew the second they did we'd file and serve.

Michael Ambarian (Supreme Court Justice)

The justice motions for another pint of Guinness Stout. I pass—I've had two already, and I have never trusted auto-drive to operate my car for me.

Carrie Marlowe did not pack the Supreme Court. It was Hillary Clinton who packed the Court. Carrie Marlowe *un*packed it.

You had a situation where three Supreme Court justices were utterly unwilling to pay even the most minimal respect to basic constitutional values. These were progressive ideologues who simply ignored the Constitution. So President Marlowe and the constitutional conservatives had a choice, and they

137

made the right one—my bias at being a direct beneficiary notwithstanding, since I received my appointment to one of the vacated seats.

In the past, progressives used to say that the Constitution was a "living document," but these progressives pronounced it dead. Literally dead.

In the *Bloomberg* gun case, they held, and I'm quoting the most offensive line, which I am particularly familiar with because I argued the case before them: "Archaic provisions and interpretations of the Constitution cannot bind the hands of Congress as it seeks to guide the progress of the nation."

Can you think of a statement more at odds with the nature of our Constitution? Those "archaic provisions and interpretations" are *expressly intended* to "bind the hands of Congress." That's *why* they are there—they are not suggestions or guidelines or vague principles to be disregarded when they become inconvenient with regard to whatever policy preference you have this week.

It was the same thing when they upheld the Internet censorship laws in *Loesch v. United States*—"The Bill of Rights is vital, but not so vital as to allow unreasonable interference with the legitimate prerogatives of government in the pursuit of social justice."

A reasonability test for the First Amendment? Unbelievable. Yet the progressive establishment cheered because it could stop pretending to observe norms and rules and the rights of its opponents and simply do what it always dreamed of doing—exercise raw power as it saw fit without limits and without constraints. After all, we constitutional conservatives were evil, wicked, immoral, or whatever foul adjective you can think of. Why, who ever could think that *we* might actually have rights worthy of constitutional protection?

And these jackasses were actually surprised when President Marlowe and her Congress went ahead and impeached them.

It was clear they had to go. I was advising the Senate majority and the leaders were reluctant to do it—no one had tried to impeach a Supreme Court justice since Samuel Chase over 200 years before. I was there when President Marlowe met with the Senate leadership and told them that they were playing a role in an informal system that was long dead. Progressives had destroyed the norms and rules that governed us, and it was not only foolish but empowering to the progressives for the Senate to try and pretend otherwise.

"Decide what kind of country you want, gentlemen?" she said. "There is one remedy for this malignancy in our politics. You have to cut out the cancer. You have to impeach them, or they win and the Constitution dies. Do you want me to follow their lead? They gave me the power as president to censor and oppress my political opponents when they gave Hillary that power. Do you want me to use it? Should I rule by executive order? The Court says that's fine too. If they stay, you've signed on to that kind of governmental power, and that's how it will be. I *will* use that power. Or you can stand up for the Constitution, impeach them, and allow me to appoint justices who will stop me and every future president. But you can't have both. You have to choose, gentlemen. We are at the fork in the road. Right leads to freedom, left leads to tyranny. So, you tell me which way we go."

I doubt President Marlowe actually would have embraced dictatorial powers if the Senate had refused her. At least I hope not—but the temptation must be great to simply outlaw opposition to your policies, and those fools had given her that power if she wished to take it. It speaks to her character that she practically begged the Senate to strip it from her.

Thankfully, they did.

They tried the three most liberal justices for violating the basic tenets of the Constitution, and all three were impeached and removed. Two of them were *literally* removed—they locked themselves in their offices and security guards physically carried them, yelling and thrashing, out of the building and dumped them on the sidewalk. For the next decade the three of them would hold pathetic mock court sessions billing themselves as the "Legitimate Supreme Court," conducting little staged hearings and issuing purported rulings that the progressive press would trumpet. Ex-justice Spitzer eventually got bored and stopped showing up—the first known instance of him choosing dignity when some other option was available—and the other two passed away soon after.

The progressives still cry about the "illegitimate coup d'état" but the Constitution, as it usually is, is quite clear. The political remedy to a Supreme Court running out of control is impeachment. Impeachment is properly difficult to accomplish, so it is rarely used, but it is there when needed. The grounds are left properly vague, so it becomes a political decision, meaning the people's representatives make the decision and are held accountable at election time. Well, at least after the Seventeenth Amendment, it's been the people's representatives. Score one point in favor of the Seventeenth. Of course, it's likely to be repealed if President Patel keeps his promise.

140   I was nominated and appointed to Justice Spitzer's seat, and I did not hesitate to actively prune back the progressive,

extra-constitutional jungle of laws my predecessors had rubber-stamped. I was called a "judicial activist," and I guess I proudly wear that label. To paraphrase Barry Goldwater, "Judicial activism in the defense of liberty is no vice, and judicial modesty in the pursuit of justice is no virtue."

Here's to Barry—the conservative Barry, of course! [*The justice raises his pint.*]

6

BIG BUSINESS

"Walmart Was Not Our Friend"

Contrary to the complaints of many critics within (and without) the movement, conservatism less redefined itself than reasserted itself during these years. One of the most important changes was how conservatism began to differentiate between "business" and "free enterprise," and how it started ridding itself of the perception (and too often the reality) that it would reflexively excuse and defend even the most shamelessly corporatist of corporations.

The conservative breakup with Walmart and other giant companies that saw government as the tool of choice for lucrative contracts and to eliminate competitors marked a turning point that opened up conservatism to a second look by millions of Americans who formerly dismissed it. At the same time, the Democrats' continued embrace of these rent-seekers became a huge propaganda target for the insurgents.

But this was only one area where conservatives made changes that both appealed to other Americans and were consistent with conservative values. Conservative support for people like the organic farmers who only wanted to sell their raw milk despite regulations pushed by the dairy industry brought in new allies, and it placed liberals in the uncomfortable position of defending the corporate-friendly status quo.

■ ■ ■

Billy Coleman (Activist)

Seventy-five years after the heyday of the hippie, Coleman is proud of his tie-dye fashion sense—and of his work with conservatives to counter the former retail juggernaut Walmart. Gesturing at a thriving mall of small shops on the outskirts of Denver, Coleman explains how conservatives' abandonment of unprincipled allies led him to join.

This used to be a Walmart. Not anymore. Walmart found itself out of friends. I remember when the Republicans were killing themselves covering for Walmart and these other big companies—just killing themselves with working people who saw what these companies did to wages and communities. Yeah, they sold cheap stuff all right, most of it crap from China. They paid nothing for stuff from the US, so that drove down wages. For conservatives, making excuses for these companies was totally counterproductive.

See, the base for conservatives was always small business, but Walmart crushed small businesses. It was poison to the people who made conservatism work. Now, some conservatives thought of Walmart as some sort of capitalist success story, and maybe it was in its first few years. But then it grew so big that it started relying on the government to shift the playing field. It supported Obamacare to shift its workers onto Uncle Sam's dime while crushing smaller competitors. It supported environmental regulations it could afford to comply with but that killed off competitors. It loved food stamps expansion—that meant more money for people to spend at its megastores.

The conservatives finally woke up to the fact that Walmart was just corporatism pretending to be free enterprise. And they stopped helping it.

Attacking Walmart was a huge step toward getting working folk to realize that conservatives were on the side of the little guy. Standing by us raw milk farmers, that was another. Hell, they made me a Republican. Can you believe it?

Dagny Eames (Libertarian Activist)

Walmart started out as a way to bring a vast array of goods at low prices to underserved markets, mostly outside the big cities. It did this by ruthlessly cutting costs and imposing efficiencies on itself and its suppliers. This was all great. But then it discovered that it was easier to hop in bed with the government than, you know, actually compete.

That was not so great.

This was a huge problem, and first the Obama and then the second Clinton administration just made it worse. Instead of fighting big business, they co-opted it. It was corporatism—corporatism where they publically slammed the people they were working hand in hand with.

Like so many giant businesses—General Motors, the banks— Walmart was a fraud, at least when it came to the issue of free

145

enterprise. It wanted to be thought of as a torchbearer of capitalism to the suckers in the GOP who never met a company they didn't like.

But Walmart and its ilk were no longer capitalist in any meaningful way—their path to success was no longer through competition and providing value but through government rent-seeking. They used their size and influence to shape the playing field so that competitors couldn't even get off the bench, much less into the end zone.

As a libertarian, this really offended me. I hated the excuses the establishment Republicans made, and I detested the "understanding" these companies had with the Democrats—if we play ball, you'll help us snuff out our competitors.

Walmart was a particularly odious example. It backed Obamacare even though that socialist fantasy was anathema to any free marketer. Why? It was good for their business. Obamacare saddled smaller competitors with huge new expenses while letting Walmart dump its workers off on the public treasury by cutting them to 29 hours per week.

And it supported green scams because it could afford to—and it knew its competitors could not. It had the capital to invest in "greening" itself, but those expenses would cripple its competitors.

Walmart even supported gun control because it wanted to corner the guns and ammo market. Small shops would be swamped by the new paperwork and record-keeping requirements, leaving only Walmart.

By the second Obama administration, it was clear that Walmart and many other corporations were no longer about competition. They were about getting the government to kill of their competition on their behalf. And in return, there was campaign money and support when the politicians—in both parties—needed it.

What was worse for constitutional conservatives was that defending Walmart alienated conservatives' natural allies, like us libertarians. The liberals Walmart sucked up to professed to hate it—they couldn't say enough bad stuff about that retail monster, or about the banks or Big Pharma or any of the other corporatist frauds. The liberals got to pose as the protectors of the little guy when they were crushing the little guy.

And the Walmarts didn't care what the liberals *said*; it cared how they voted, and the liberal politicians always went the way of their corporate allies in the end. So it ended up that the Republicans, including some conservatives, defended Walmart, thinking it was an ally, even as Walmart undercut everything conservatives believe in.

The thing is that the corporatists like Walmart were bringing ruin upon the working class by exporting jobs and driving down wages at home and then devastating the small business owners who formed the core of conservatism in America.

In other words, conservatives were too often siding with a liberal-aligned group that was wrecking the conservatives' base. And all in the name of "free enterprise" that was hardly free and less an enterprise than a racket.

And if that was not bad enough, Walmart and other corporatists acted like a huge vacuum cleaner, sucking up the free money the government was handing out by expressly targeting the EBT card–wielding welfare cheat demographic. You didn't see many Walmarts in affluent areas—you saw them where there are plenty of folks getting government dollars that could be spent in their megastores. And Walmart had no desire to see that particular well run dry.

147

Sure, it would occasionally try some public relations stunt, like promising crappy jobs to veterans. Awesome. For the "price" of getting a bunch of accomplished, responsible, drug-free individuals, Walmart got to look like this great corporate citizen where, in reality, it was embodying every stereotype of a corporate scourge.

As a libertarian, I used to like Walmart in theory. I thought it was a great American capitalist success story. Being a largely urban woman, I had only been to Walmart a couple of times. But then I saw that Walmart was everything wrong with American politics and a wonderful example of "free enterprise" that made its profits by, through, and from tax money stolen from the people who actually produce something.

The night the government checks arrived became payday for losers. It was party time in dependency city, and Walmart was there, ready to skim off that sweet, sweet government cash.

It was my money and your money at work. Or, more accurately, not at work. More like our pocket being picked and Walmart eagerly taking a cut.

So what could we do? The first thing we needed to do was take the blinders off. I'll modestly take credit on behalf of the libertarians who became constitutional conservatives, but we started making the people in the movement aware that big companies were not necessarily part of the solution. Conservatives had been defending business for so long that they didn't notice that many of the companies they defended had defected to the other side and were now part of the problem.

What was wrong with Walmart—its shameless corporatism, its rent-seeking, its embrace of the welfare state as a way to ensure its clientele has the dough to spend on cut-rate crap imported from Asia while crushing our core constituencies here at home—was pretty much the same as what was wrong with most businesses that you can stick the word "big" in front of.

They may have been companies, but they weren't capitalist and they sure as hell weren't conservative. Conservatives protected them because they didn't see what the corporatists had truly become: part of the problem. In fact, they weren't just part of the problem but active participants in worsening the problem.

See, progressivism was not a problem to these companies. Big government, regulation, entitlements—they *wanted* these things. They *liked* them.

So when conservatives defended them, conservatives were defending people who were not only working against conservative interests but against conservatism's core constituencies. And conservatives let the left pretend to hate them.

Step one was to stop defending them. Walmart and the big corporations could take care of themselves—hell, they'd been taking care of themselves at our expense for decades. We needed to untie and uncouple conservatism from these rent-seeking rackets. That meant we needed to call them out—hard and loud.

And we did. Suddenly, constitutional conservatives were offering a critique of corporatist business. The establishment GOP, of course, hated this. The corporations immediately allied with them to fund pliable, controllable candidates to fight constitutional conservatives in the GOP primaries. They poured money into the fight through the consultant class. There was one problem—the establishment had most of the money, but we constitutional conservatives had most of the actual Republican voters.

Step two was that we took advantage of the alliances and opportunities that treating these corporate hacks just as badly as they treat us could offer. There was a whole strata of society that had been screwed by them, people who held us in contempt because they thought we were to blame. In reality, the liberals loved the big companies that happily aided and abetted them in order to ensure their profits through government action. They just hid their secret love affair behind propaganda talking about how liberals were somehow the champions of the little guys the liberals were shafting.

It shouldn't be a surprise, but we conservatives love small things more than big things. Name one small thing liberals like, besides a small military? Sure, they hate "big" stuff. My ass.

And step three, as our power increased, we pushed for new laws that leveled the playing field for our constituencies. In the macro sense, as we shrank government we naturally shrank the incentive to focus their business models on rent-seeking since we eliminated the potential to win in Washington rather than in the marketplace. When government did less, there was less to be gained from lobbying. They had to refocus back on actually earning business rather than paying K Street hacks to win them special government favors.

We also focused on targeted reforms that addressed some structural inequities. Small businesses already got slammed with higher individual tax rates because most small business owners paid taxes as individuals, while companies got lower rates. We fixed that. There were dozens of other subsidies, scams, and scandals that these rackets took advantage of. We rooted them out too, and we let the liberals fight to preserve corporate welfare. Which they obliged us by doing.

In fact, we kicked the corporatists off the dole before we did it to individuals. That helped show America we were serious. The liberals freaked out even as we paid back the traitors to free enterprise.

Trevor Gore (Stand-Up Comic)

We are in the green room of Atlantic City's Boardwalk Giggle Works, a comedy club that is currently in the midst of one of the periodic stand-up comedy crazes that have been occurring on and off for nearly half a century. We can see snow falling outside the dirty window. On a stained couch, veteran comic Trevor Gore gestures wildly with a cigarette in his right hand and a glass of Jack Daniels in his left—listening to his staccato delivery, even in one-on-one conversation with him, you worry that you will be splashed or burned, or possibly both. "I'm related to Al Gore—remember him?" he shouts, although I'm two feet away "The guy who was into global warming? Remember that scam? It's freaking six degrees outside!"

Gore is a pro who can fill a room with fans even on a weeknight, but then he has been doing his shtick for nearly 30 years. He had gone to Columbia to be a doctor, but instead of studying he spent his nights at the smoke-free comedy clubs of Michael Bloomberg's New York City before quitting school entirely for life before the faux brick wall.

"I hated Bloomberg, that little fascist prick," he says, "but then the city elects that socialist ass wipe de Blasio and it's like *Lord of the Flies*. I mean, the whole place goes to hell. I thought I was a lefty, like all my friends, but I wasn't blind. I didn't buy that I had to get mugged so socialism could triumph. Count me out."

Gore began turning his wit on the icons and shibboleths of the left largely out of sheer contrariness. "Everyone was afraid to make jokes about these tools. I wasn't, and I caught all sorts of shit for it."

He lost gigs in 2016 because he refused to hide the fact that he wouldn't vote for Hillary Clinton. By 2018 his act was overtly political, and his explicitly conservative-oriented comedy album, *Right Up Yours*, broke him through to young people dispirited by a decade of progressive malaise. While he was merciless to politicians, he had

151

a special enmity toward large businesses that collaborated with the progressives to milk the system.

"I did a long bit on that album about a visit to a Walmart I made when I was on tour in Atlanta in 2017. And I saw that the store was designed entirely to take money from the people the government had just given it to. No wonder these companies were funding progressives—the welfare money went right into their pockets after a few hours in the pockets of the welfare bums." Performances like Gore's, and other like-minded comedians, gave mass audiences permission to be angry at the takers in society—and at companies that enabled them.

Though his "My Visit to Walmart" bit became the climax of his live shows for several years, it got his album banned from Walmart's shelves. "Of course," he says, "Amazon was very happy to promote it!"

Now, I take 81 milligrams of baby aspirin every night because my doctor says it might keep my heart from exploding. So, I'm on a trip to Atlanta and I had forgotten my baby aspirin, right? So, I look around and the only place nearby is this enormous Walmart super-ultra-mega store. It's literally a choice between dying of a heart attack and going into this Walmart on welfare check night, and I'm not sure I chose right.

I pull up into the parking lot and it's clear everyone there is on some kind of welfare. How do I know? I'm from New York. I know what a loser looks like. These were not career-focused individuals, okay?

So, the parking lot is packed with cars. This disturbed me, because people who get government money should not have cars. Okay, they should sell their cars to buy the things that my tax money is buying them. Otherwise, that really means that I'm subsidizing their cars and as far as I am concerned, cars are for closers. No work-work, no vroom-vroom.

Of course, I would solve that problem of people using their government money on things I don't approve of, like cars for losers, by ending all government programs. See, if it isn't any of my money, then it isn't any of my concern. But I digress.

Now, I want to be clear that I'm not somehow "better than Walmart" or the normal people who patronize it. There were a few normals that night. You could tell them because they were as scared as I was. But I am, however, significantly better than the loafing losers who descended on the welfare money magnet of a store that night.

You are also better than them. I don't even know you and I'm very comfortable saying that.

So, I decide I've gotta get my aspirin. How bad can it be, right? I work my way through the throng to the main entrance. And it's full of sketchy people. There should have been a sign reading "Welcome to Walmart. Please, no sudden moves."

My clean clothes, my combed hair, my general air of self-sufficiency . . . these pegged me as a figure due awe and respect. The other shoppers gave me a wide berth, which was good since many of them were pretty damn wide themselves.

Do not get me going on how America is full of fat people on food stamps.

So, I'd never been in a Walmart before. I'm from New York. If a store's bigger than my living room I start getting agoraphobia. Anyway, the interior was like an aircraft hangar filled with five supermarkets, and it's illuminated with the glow of a hundred fluorescent lights way up on the ceiling. The sheer size and variety inside was amazing, and that was just the people.

The aisles were about twice as wide as those in any other store

153

I'd ever been in. Like I said, in America obesity is a disease that correlates with being "poor."

Of course "poor" is a relative term. When you talk about people overseas, "poor" would mean, roughly, "no money." But these folks, that night, had money all right—my money and your money. So, in America, the term "poor" apparently refers not to the amount of money one has but, rather, whether or not one gets it from Uncle Sam in return for voting for liberal Democrats.

I noticed a bunch of "poor" people hustling their new big screens up to the front counter. They were happy to get the money that afternoon, and Walmart was happy to relieve them of it that evening.

Yeah, look for Walmart to be all in for entitlement cuts.

The customers that night were a United Nations of all races and ethnicities united by the promise of consumer spending subsidized by others who actually work for a living.

They seemed calmed by the crackling fluorescent lights and soothing colors of the displays. This was not just a place to shop for material goods but a kind of temple to Deadbeato, the wrathful god of entitlements.

It creeped me out.

I start walking toward where they sell the medicine, and then I realize that I have no idea where they sell the medicine. Could be in the next state, the place is so big.

I look for an employee. Nearby, there's one Walmart guy surrounded by eight blaze-orange cones using a sheet of cardboard to fan a purple spill on the linoleum like it's the pharaoh. He looks scared.

"Hey, where's the medicine aisle?" I ask. He looks at me dead-eyed, but keeps on fanning. It's fun to confuse people by speaking to them clearly in proper English, but I try it another way.

"Dude, medicine aisle? Hello?"

He stops fanning for a second, points a dirty finger vaguely off into the distance, and then goes back to fanning the puddle.

I go in that direction. To my right was a big DVD promotion for an upcoming Dwayne "the Rock" Johnson movie. Yeah, he used to really throw a wrench into my Oscar handicapping. I was thinking that they must be bracing themselves for the rush when the Shakespeare box set comes out.

So, I'm walking through the store and these clumps of people are moving to and fro among the aisles. Apparently, the clientele's fashion watchword is "tight." Yeah, when in doubt, cut off the blood supply to your lower half.

I think that there must be a special clothing size above XXXL called "Walmart."

I learned that spandex is the devil's fabric. I still wonder how muumuus could be form fitting.

If you're ever in a Walmart on welfare check night, and you shouldn't be, watch out! Rascal scooters have the right of way! I had no idea so many people were mobility-challenged, and no idea why so many of these riders were about my age. Most of them are immobile because they are just too massive.

I guess whatever government program was giving them free go-carts on my dime decided that the cure for getting too little exercise was to get none at all.

Well, honking their little horns at us losers who actually walked, like suckers, was a kind of exercise, I guess. Feel the burn in that thumb!

I passed the greeting cards aisle. It had sections of cards designed for "Fathers" and "Grandfathers," but they really needed one for "That Random Dude Who Shacked Up With Mom." I didn't stop to inspect the bizarre familial arrangements acknowledged by the greeting card cartel. The best measure of the spread of social pathologies is your local Hallmark display.

There was an astonishing variety of foot-related products. Apparently feet are very important to people who rarely get up off the couch and onto them.

I swear I saw a tumbleweed bouncing down the lonely, deserted dental hygiene products aisle.

A lot of people were doing a lot of scratching. I've rarely been so happy that a place requires pants.

The forklift rumbled through to deliver a crate to the pharmacy. It read "Valtrex." I didn't use the water fountain.

The skin care aisle was packed. If government has to get involved, it should mandate that Walmart sell a cream that fights both chronic acne and chronic sloth.

There was a wide variety of birth control products, but judging from the number of little urchins running around, no one used them. Walmart could have made a fortune selling at-home paternity tests.

Here's a helpful observation: moms, dads, maybe your precocious 13-year-old daughter ought not to be wearing shorts with the word "Juicy" emblazoned across her ass.

Now, if you have to ask me why that's a bad idea, okay, she's probably pregnant already.

Congrats—you're on your way to being a 39-year-old great grandma.

So, eventually, I get to the medicine aisle. I will say this—300 low-dose aspirins for $3.99 is a killer buy. Love those Malaysian pharmaceutical companies and their rock bottom prices!

Time to make a break for it. But I made a few more observations on the way out.

I'd never seen so many unironic mullets. You know, Unironic Mullets would be a great band name. Not that these folks would be fans of the Unironic Mullets' alternative proto-fuzz guitar skronk. Their T-shirts let me know many were fans of rappers I'd never heard of like Killa Z, or terrible nü metal bands with names like Blaaklyst. It would have been a great venue for a Limp Bizkit reunion concert.

There's nothing like a label assuring you that your cheese product is "Made with Real Cheese." I found myself pondering the question, "Who buys a gallon jug of Utz Cheese Balls?" Anyway, I soon found out. Okay, let me put it this way: some questions you just don't want answered.

I also found out from watching one elderly gentleman that if you're lonely, you can have a chat with the ATM. A long chat. With questions. And, apparently, it will answer you back.

Yeah, the goth trailer park look many of the folks were rockin' was awesome. Here's another idea that popped into my head: when thinking about tatting up your whole arm, understand that someday you'll be 80. Unless, of course, you want that barbed wire ring around your bicep to fade over time into a Dada-esque blur.

At the counter, I watched a clerk say, "No, EBT don't work for Night Train." The disappointed customer should have known that, since he had clearly never actually had any real money.

Another highlight was the guy with "666" tattooed on his neck trying to cash a personal check without ID. He seemed legit. I mean, in comparison.

I paid with a credit card, which seemed to freak the checker out. He asked for my ID, and when I had some it freaked him out even more.

The whole time, everyone seemed to be on the verge of asking me, "You a cop?"

When I walked out of there, I felt like I just left an off-Broadway production of *Megan's List*.

You've been a great audience! Good night!

7

THE SAFE HAVEN OF THE STATES

"They Were Our Liberated Territory"

Conservatism was rising, and it faced enemies not only on the left but from "moderate" Republicans more concerned with losing their personal influence than in pushing conservative policies. Though the conservatives took over the GOP by 2020, the third party campaign (aided and abetted by rich liberals and disenfranchised Republican establishment veterans) of a "moderate" GOP defector was sufficient to allow Hillary Clinton a second term with a pathetic 39% of the vote while the Democrats held the Senate. But the states were another matter, and it was from this base that they moved toward a 2024 presidential victory.

■ ■ ■

Colonel Jeremy Denton, US Army (Ret.)
(Insurgency Expert)

Nothing succeeds like success, and one of the keys to a successful insurgency is successfully governing in the liberated areas outside the control of the powerful central government. You have to demonstrate that the alternative works or the people—who are what you need to be focused on—won't be with you.

We had that in our insurgency. We had the red states with conservative governors showing that we weren't incompetent, and at the same time letting us build strength for the fight. They were our liberated territory.

Tamara Hayes Smith (Professor/Activist)

Thanks to the wisdom of the Founders and their recognition of the sovereignty of the states, we had an essential sanctuary where conservative ideas could flourish. And, critically, it demonstrated to a dubious national electorate that the constitutional conservatives were competent and capable of governing.

Our opponents faced a daunting problem because the states we controlled—a slight majority—continued to improve and prosper while their blue state neighbors continued to spin around the toilet bowl, awaiting the inevitable moment when their profligate spending pulled them down the drain. The Illinois bankruptcy was one example—Hillary bailed it out, which cost her greatly politically because it was so unpopular, but then California followed and that was much worse.

Look at California, hamstrung by its own liberal incoherence. The rich liberals on the coast who controlled it, with the assent of the mass of poor and generally hopeless, had managed to take a state packed with incredible riches and essentially write off any industry that focused on exploiting those resources. California guzzled power, but it outsourced the dirty work of generating that power out of state. So red states that did use their resources got paid by California, a state with even greater, but untouched, resources.

California was a huge engine for growth and opportunities, but liberalism didn't just kill the goose that laid the golden egg. It killed the whole flock. By the 2010s, what manufacturers remained in California (they had been leaving in droves for a decade already) faced new and even more ridiculous rules designed to address the global warming scam. These rules crushed manufacturing and transportation sectors and drove them east. The Golden State, suffocating under unfunded pension liabilities for an army of do-nothing, layabout government drones and run by and for the benefit of their unions, was pretty much doomed.

Who wanted to come to California? The drive into the state over the crumbling freeways was tough enough but once you got there, there was nothing for you. There were no jobs, and the land use rules limited housing so there was hardly any to be had without paying a king's ransom. But even if you managed to earn a king's ransom, it was taken from you by some of the highest taxes in the country.

California became a state with a huge number of welfare recipients, a few megamillionaires, and a dwindling middle class. That was a recipe for disaster.

If you were young and wanted to succeed, you had to go someplace like Texas. Low taxes, a reasonable standard of living, fewer plaintiff lawyers. Sure, for a while California dominated a few industries, but emerging technology meant industries like high tech and entertainment could function seamlessly anywhere. Is it any wonder these businesses went where they treated business well—the conservative states?

Hollywood became less a center of production than the place movie stars came back to after shooting their projects elsewhere so the paparazzi could find them and give them free publicity.

Now, a lot of people in this country weren't very bright—look at how they voted. However, few were insane. Some people voted for Democrats in the blue states because they actually thought that liberal governance worked. But many were also willing to change their minds when they compared disasters like Obamacare at the federal level and the blue state bankruptcies with good, solid governance in red states like Utah and Texas. The liberal partisans were actually a fairly small group, a hard core of maybe 20 percent of the population. The rest of the people who voted for liberals were the ones the liberals could only fool some of the time.

Sure, the blue states resisted change. They had to—for many liberals, government paid the bills. In California, they had to see the Four Horsemen of the Liberal Apocalypse galloping down Sunset Boulevard to reform.

Now, in the meantime, those banjo-strumming barbarians in the Lone Star State were raking in the cash. People weren't blind. They picked up on things like success—especially when they saw their tax money siphoned away to provide babysitting services for the illegitimate children of struggling performance artists. Seriously, that happened. And conservatives in California made a huge deal about it when they were fighting to turn the Golden State red again.

Providing a virtuous example to contrast with the cautionary example of the blue states was just one key function of the conservative states. Another was to be the vaunted laboratories of democracy we heard so much about in high school government courses. Bobby Jindal and other governors were out there cooking up all sorts of ideas—like eliminating the income tax—that were blueprints for success elsewhere. And successes in the red states made reform at the federal level easier—there was a track record of success our candidates could point to.

There was another benefit—the farm team. The GOP was plagued with far too many candidates who couldn't seem to generate the intellectual wattage of a pile of used car batteries. Those geniuses were a real problem. The states offered a great training ground for new talent—and a way to separate the quality wheat from the chaff.

Then there was the matter of the power to make law at the state level. This was huge. Remember, we were in a cultural struggle, and much of it took place at the local level. We conservatives started with some of the obvious stuff. The basis of a conservative society is marriage and family. The feds wanted to tear those institutions apart—they're a huge enemy to those who want to remake mankind. So we doubled down on supporting them at the state level.

The liberals wanted single-parent families. Back from the Marxist/Frankfurt School days, the left had an ideological predisposition to hate traditional families—they saw them as vehicles of resistance to state power. They also rightly saw them as institutions that reinforced conservative values. Poll after poll showed that Democrats had huge support from single mothers, for example, while marriage and family correlated with the GOP. Liberals wanted to take the place of fathers and husbands. We had to reverse that.

We reformed taxes and other benefits to favor married couples starting in the states. Later, we would bring these reforms

163

to the federal level. We wanted the default condition for adults to be half of a married couple instead of being hungover man-children who spent their days playing *Call of Duty* video games and watching Internet porn. Conservatives increased the tax deductions for married couples, eliminated marriage penalties, and actually set a marriage advantage. Then they added tax credits for kids.

This sounds kind of harsh to those singles, but why should immaturity be subsidized? We wanted young people to move on from adolescence, not have the people who did grow up bankroll those who wouldn't. It was and is the families who make the country run, not the players and bimbos who enjoyed the benefits of a stable society they undercut. Plus, since singles tended to vote for Democrats, conservatives felt that when it comes to choosing who gets screwed, choose the other side.

It was called hardball. The conservatives learned that lesson well after having the Obama administration jam liberalism down its throat on straight party line votes. They learned to reward their friends and punish their enemies. A lot of liberals very sadly reaped what they had sown once Carrie Marlowe was elected.

And the states were a great place to pursue our struggle against various institutions that had joined up with liberals to shaft our society. Universities were a very inviting target. Many depended on state governments, and it never occurred to them that those conservative state governments might not feel like continuing to subsidize the liberal tumors in their midst. They had to adapt, meaning turn rightward or starve. They chose not to starve.

Trial lawyers were another funding source for the left. The red states found that tort reform was not only good policy but a great way to starve the plaintiffs' bar. When that big trial lawyer had a cash crunch and had to choose between another diamond for Mrs. Third Wife and sending a check to the Democratic National Committee, guess who got paid?

And the red state governments targeted the unions, those evergreen funders of liberal pathologies. Michigan and Indiana became right-to-work states early on. Others followed. This dried up Democratic funding in the red states but also had the effect of making unionization less competitive in the blue states. After all, when their businesses couldn't compete, the unions would go under. And every time a union shop closed its doors, the Democrats got weaker and the conservatives got stronger.

Oh, and the red state bans on public employee unions were a huge victory. Banning them cut costs, improved the schools, and crippled the Democrats. It was political advantage overlapping good policy. The federal government followed suit—President Marlowe signed the law ending the right of federal employees to unionize.

They also wisely locked in their success with improvements to election security. The liberals used to scream bloody murder about voter ID, as if millions of voters couldn't come up with identification. It was a scam—they needed, desperately, the ability to cheat. Voter ID helped stop that. So did tougher penalties for voter fraud, with an increased focus on the inner city elections where most election fraud happened.

The conservatives were pretty ruthless once they took control, but they had learned their lesson. If you don't fight to win, you fight to lose, and this was political warfare. Successful insurgents can't waste time playing patty-cake.

Tony "Gator" McCoy (Chief Advisor to President Carrie Marlowe)

Marlowe, advised by McCoy, first came to prominence in her fights with the Clinton administration over federal gun laws. The Anti-Violence Control Act sought to limit private ownership of weapons following the newly majority liberal Supreme Court's ruling that there was no individual right to keep and bear arms. This decision, *Bloomberg v. NRA*, was overturned by the Thirtieth Amendment in 2028, reaffirming the fundamental right of mentally competent, law-abiding citizens to carry weapons for the defense of themselves, their family, their community, and the Constitution.

As Florida's governor, Carrie Marlowe stunned the political world by snagging the GOP nomination in 2024. She made no bones about her constitutional conservatism. None, and that was something new. No more establishment losers getting the GOP nomination. We constitutional conservatives had finally reached the big game.

As governor, she slashed the Florida state budget while other states teetered on the edge of bankruptcy, and she slashed taxes as well. Just chopped it. We called Florida "an island of common-sense prosperity in a sea of liberal despair" in our ads. Drove the libs nuts. She also built a coalition of citizens concerned about personal liberty by suing the feds over the Obamacare health info leaks against Clinton opponents in Florida.

And she royally pissed off Hillary by refusing to allow any Florida agency to cooperate with the feds in enforcing the Anti-Violence Control Act. It didn't get as bad as it did in Texas, thank God, but it was a defining moment. Yeah, Hillary hated her, so Carrie knew she was doing all right!

Sandy Crawford (Conservative Activist)

Say you lived in California, and you're being taxed to support a dependent class while prices are going up because of regulations and your dreams for you and your family are denied. Then, you look across the border at Arizona and it is everything California is not—prosperous, free, a place of opportunity—and, moreover, conservatives are constantly pointing that out.

Eventually, the contradictions get heightened, and combined with a real effort at grassroots organization to take back the GOP, suddenly conservatism became viable again even in the bluest states.

Roberta Klein (Conservative Activist/Attorney)

We tied Obamacare up in knots, and with help from conservative state governments that refused to cooperate, we set the stage for repeal.

State governments were key, creating state laws that allowed us to litigate for conservative change at the state level. New university diversity and free speech laws allowed faculty and students to go to court more effectively to challenge progressive campus speech codes, unfair disciplinary codes, and discrimination against conservatives. These spurred huge changes.

Before, that kind of petty progressive tyranny was cost-free. Now, a winning student or aspiring faculty member could go to state court and win not only an injunction but substantial money damages and attorney's fees. With the states giving us these tools, we could start the larger cultural fight.

Darcy Mizuhara McCullough (Former Missouri Governor)

That I was the first Asian-American governor of Missouri, and a woman, just made the liberals crazy. They were offended that I wasn't buying into what they were selling. Why would I? I could see the results. California used to be the Golden State, but companies were leaving there as fast as they could pack. The only folks left were people on welfare and super rich liberals.

Oh, they were furious when I'd run ads in Los Angeles and Chicago and in the Bay Area telling companies to come to Missouri. Our slogan was, "Missouri: We Appreciate You." They hated it. I loved it! And we never let up on them.

When I was running, I told Missourians to look around, that they had a choice. They could make this a booming red state like Texas or Louisiana, or go down the drain like blue California and Illinois. They looked, and they chose red and me!

•We used the Republican Governors Association as a way to exchange ideas about new policies and reforms, and we worked with think tanks and grassroots groups to develop them and share them. You saw liberal Washington trying to increase taxes, and blue states too, while we cut them. We pushed right-to-work laws and reformed government employment practices in our states, and things improved.

The voters in the blue states started wondering why they were falling behind, and then they started to see that in blue states the governments were by, for, and about public employee unions and entitlement recipients. And they started to get tired of it. Who wants to slave away at a job to make sure some DMV clerk who retired at 42 gets another $200 a month in his pension?

We also gerrymandered—hell, we redistricted mercilessly in 2020. We learned from liberals that this game was for keeps,

168

and that's how we played. See, at first we could only play defense in DC, but in the states we could grow and learn and prove ourselves and conservatism to the American people, who had frankly started to doubt us. Having safe havens in the states was critical to our comeback.

What was most important about having the states was the comparison it provided, our success through conservatism versus their blue failure. Sure, the media tried to poke holes in what we were doing—*60 Minutes* must have done a dozen sob stories on how mean we were to poor people. Except it backfired on them.

They thought they had me when I was interviewed about "hungry people without jobs" in St. Louis and I said, "If you won't work, you *should* be hungry. You need to go out and support yourself." My ratings went up eight points the week after that aired!

8

BIG MONEY

"A Few Rich Guys Made a Huge Difference"

Much of the heavy lifting of the conservative insurgency was done by regular people acting in their own communities, but the contributions of a number of wealthy businessmen—not only in terms of cash but in business savvy and contacts—helped the movement tremendously. Liberals fixated on these "suspicious donors," and many found themselves targeted by activists, the media, and even government bureaucrats for daring to confront the establishment.

■ ■ ■

Dan Stringer (Billionaire CEO/Activist)

The vilified tycoon is outspoken about his views and how he went for the throat against the liberal establishment that hated him.

The leftists used to say that our dad, and then me and my brother, bought and paid for the entire conservative revival. But I think our contribution was less in quantity than quality. We used a rigorous cost-benefit approach—where could we spend money to maximize our return? We sought the most bang for the buck, as it were.

Some of the big conservative institutions—think tanks, magazines, and other groups—had gotten fat and lazy on easy money from big donors. We demanded measurable results. I remember one bunch of consultants wanted a zillion bucks for some technological get-out-the-vote program. The guy had a wonderful presentation using the latest software—holograms and everything. My brother Dave vectored in a couple of software guys to analyze the plan. It was shit. We passed. Some other rich guy funded it. A great presentation and then a million bucks, down the toilet.

I used to think, "Hell, if you want to give away a million bucks for nothing, I'll do nothing for $500,000. You can't pass up that deal!" No takers, though.

Look, the rich guys who liked to spend money on conservative causes were indispensable to the movement, but they just needed to be as wise about the conservative groups they invested in as they were about their business decisions. They didn't get rich in business pouring money into bottomless pits without a strategy nor any accountability, yet that's what they did when they handed over huge stacks of cash to folks whose only demonstrated competence was in the fine art of failure.

There was this vast array of Republican—not necessarily conservative—consultants, institutes, publications, and other scams devoted to separating rich conservatives from their dough. Most of them fought real conservatives until they saw we were winning. Then they acted like they had been with us every step of the way. I remembered who had been there from the beginning, but some donors forgot. They got hosed; I got my payback.

I tried to tell people in my circles that they needed to think about what they were doing and how they were spending their money. The movement was about more than some huckster's new Mercedes.

Using money effectively takes thought—it's easy to write a big check but hard to write a bunch of little ones. We made the effort. When it came to giving, we started by thinking small. The Internet as we know it was less than 20 years old when Obama was reelected, and social media was still a new thing. We were just discovering how it could work, how it could be used to link and coordinate and motivate people for action.

But a lot of wealthy donors didn't pay attention to it—you didn't get rich blogging or tweeting or Facebooking or Tumblring. So they didn't see them as important. But they were important to real people—you know, the kind who actually vote?

There were zillions of regular conservatives promoting conservatism with those tools, and none of them had any money. We wondered what the most talented ones could do with a few bucks, and that guided our microgiving.

Now, you could write some guy a $750,000 check after a flashy Holo-PowerPoint presentation—well, back then it was just 2D PowerPoint, but you know what I mean—about how his software was going to revolutionize get-out-the-vote efforts and get a big, fat goose egg. On the other hand, you could get one of your minions to parcel out 10 grand at a time, which was real money to starving Internet activists, to find would-be investigative journalists to go and get video of liberals messing up.

Remember ACORN? For a small investment in a pimp suit, a couple young conservatives took out a huge arm of the Democratic Party. That pimp suit is now on display in the Stringer Hall of Modern American Political History at the Smithsonian, by the way.

How about hiring a few young attorneys? The market was saturated and young ones with a lot of energy, but not much experience, were willing to work all night for nearly nothing just to get into a courtroom. Unleashing the ambulance chasers was the modern equivalent of releasing the hounds.

You would weigh costs versus benefits in your business life, but we did it in our conservative giving. Sure, most of these microgrants didn't generate any value. As in all areas of human endeavor, most ideas were crap. But some weren't, and the value to the movement far exceeded our relatively paltry investment. Plus we were training these folks, letting them get experience. As they got better, they could do more damage to progressivism down the road.

See, notice how I called it an "investment"? I expected a return on investment. For the price of one big failure, a single rich guy could energize scores of young, eager conservatives who wanted to use new media to carry the fight to the enemy. Keep in mind that, unlike the consultants, these were true believers. You gave them some seed money to buy a decent laptop or a working camera, and they would more than match your money with their own sweat equity.

With them, it was like lighting a fuse. With the consultants, it was filling up their gas tank, and when the tank ran dry the car got parked in the garage. We leveraged the dedication, creativity, and initiative of these conservative activists. That was a savvy play.

Second, after thinking smaller, we started thinking *bigger*. We asked ourselves why we should toss another chunk of change into some obscure magazine read only by a bunch of bow tie–wearing weenies? The *National Review, Weekly Standard,* and *American Spectator* are all useful and essential, and they needed money—which we gave—but how much use was some in-house compendium of think tank fellows' scribbling? Sure, I know I loved to catch up on what some otherwise unemployable Georgetown political science grad thought about urban housing policy. Who didn't? Well, pretty much everyone.

The conservative movement didn't need more venues for pointless pontificating by sexless policy nerds—that's what we called them then, nerds. Instead, the movement needed to communicate conservative values and conservative solutions to real people who actually voted, not people who loved to sit around and trade about DC bar gossip.

We decided to dive into general interest publications, the ones real people read—especially women, who were being fed this endless stream of liberal propaganda. We made offers to buy women's magazines like *Redbook* and *Cosmopolitan* that you would see at the supermarket checkout stands back then. They would have these ridiculous articles like "Summer Beach Bikini Secrets for the Busy Mom" or "10 Super-Sexy Ways to Please Your Man . . . Including One That Requires a Vacuum Cleaner!" but in between was this default liberal fluff. We wanted to insert our own conservative fluff.

The big magazines wouldn't sell out to us because we were conservative. They should have—they're all bankrupt now, and their names live on as websites after being auctioned by their bankruptcy trustees.

We bought some of the smaller ones whose owners weren't as lockstep liberal and who wanted to get a few bucks out ahead

175

of the industry's final death throes. Others we bought through front companies to hide our identities.

I made no bones about "editorial independence"—we put solid conservatives at the wheel. Soon, you'd see things like a profile of a conservative woman politician that didn't treat her like someone Hitler would tell to chill out.

We'd offer some practical personal safety hints for women—like how to buy the right handgun. Boy, that freaked people out, but regular women had never seen that side of things before—they came expecting recipes and celebrity gossip and got a fresh perspective, a conservative perspective, painlessly and without fanfare. Sure, the liberal political rags were in a tizzy at us usurping their dominance, but the women weren't reading those liberal magazines!

We didn't sell it as overt conservatism—why turn off our audience by being overt? Instead, we made huge gains off of "good government" exposés on how bureaucrats squandered the money the readers' families paid in taxes. We'd even wedge in an occasional piece on a woman who didn't like abortion. You'd never see that reading *Woman's Day*.

We also bought men's magazines, and we irritated some on our side by keeping the photos of sexy starlets cavorting in lingerie. Conservative men like hot women, and they're proud of it. We just added some conservative content. Our men's mags loved to profile hard-core studs—SEALs, football players, and that sort of thing. To that we'd add some explicit coverage of their largely conservative views—there are not a lot of progressive SEALs. Badassary and liberalism are, after all, mutually exclusive.

176 But why stop at magazines? We began to think even *bigger*. How about a video network?

Back in 2009, on the right, serving half of America's 300-some odd million people was Fox News. That is all.

There was a huge opportunity there. Glenn Beck saw it and founded TheBlaze TV network from scratch, though that was an entirely different animal than buying a going concern. It was a risk. He became a zillionaire, but he could have easily found himself wearing a barrel.

We didn't see this as purely charity; it was a way to potentially make a ton of dough while also helping to pop the political pimple that was progressivism. There was a huge opening that needed to be filled. Conservatives could turn on their old TV sets and have the choice of Fox News or a test pattern.

As awesome as Fox News was—and it was awesome, as anyone conscious and fighting liberalism in the dark times before Fox can attest—a lack of competition never makes the monopolist better. Monopolies will always get ossified, slower, and generally worse. That's just how things are. The *best* thing that could happen to Fox was another voice on the right. We did that. We did well with NewsRight, but Fox reigns supreme.

I think our mistake at the beginning was using "right" in the name, but I was outvoted! We should have chosen a neutral name.

Next, we thought, why stop at news? Why not popular entertainment? If we wanted to change America, we had to change the culture. If we wanted to change the culture, we would have to participate in the culture, and popular entertainment was a huge part of it.

With the old model of centralized distribution dying in an age of digital movies and video on demand and all sorts of other venues, and with production costs dropping as the insatiable appetite for material grew, it was never easier or cheaper to get into the movie and TV business. And some of us conservatives invested. A few rich guys made a huge difference. And some of us made money too.

I would tell my rich guy friends, "Everyone wants your money. The movement needs your money. Stop just giving your money away. Demand results. Monitor the metrics. If your spending isn't getting results, stop spending on the failure and start funding something else. It isn't that hard. Remember how you got rich in the first place? Remember how you did it?"

Then I would tell them, "Do that again."

Darren Dolby (Lawyer/Activist)

This well-known and flamboyant attorney represented some of the movement's wealthy donors in lawsuits after government officials decided to try and intimidate them.

You know the old saying about not getting in a pissing contest with a guy who buys ink by the barrel? There's a second part that gets less play: "Don't screw with a guy who buys lawyers by the bushel."

See that classic 2020 Corvette outside? I bought that new with part of the payoff after I hit the IRS and a bunch of its flunkies for $3,000,000 for auditing my client because he dared do what the Constitution allowed him to do and tell Hillary to go pound sand. I don't like these damn modern electric cars, so I kept it—though it's a bitch finding a gas station anymore!

9

THE NEWS

"It's Our Media Now"

The conservative insurgency was never just about politics but about the entire culture, and the media was the voice and expression of that culture. Conservatives made a conscious effort to move into the news media. As more and more journalists chaffed under the politically correct constraints of the liberal establishment, and as technology allowed new entrants in the media to bypass the established gatekeepers, the media became more conservative. And the effects on society were pronounced.

■ ■ ■

David Chang (Conservative Media Host)

Chang's snarling terrier interrupts our discussion to demand his master's attention. In the other room, Chang's husband, Luke, a high-end carpenter who makes expensive designer furniture, is fixing lunch. The enormous house—Chang has done incredibly well as a talk show host—is impeccably decorated. We are in what they call their "Gun Room." The name is apt—the walls are covered with firearms of all makes and sizes.

"They're all functional, of course," Chang tells me. "Since we don't have kids, some of them are loaded. When I was younger, every once in a while punks might try and beat up a gay couple, so I took my protection seriously. I still do. I never got why gays would back people who wanted to keep them vulnerable. Of course, I couldn't keep my mouth shut about that either and it just made them hate me more. I had to break through prejudice all right—about my conservatism. I knew I wanted to be in media, and it was pretty clear if I wanted to do that I needed to do it myself."

I was a traitor because I thought for myself. So I said, "The hell with it," and started an Internet show. It was right during the 2016 election season. I was a Chris Christie guy, though soon I became one of his biggest critics. He had spent years telling the Tea Partiers "screw you," and so no one should have been surprised when, on primary election night in Iowa, they returned the favor. Of course, then he got mad, quit the GOP when it was clear there was no place for him, and ran in 2020 as an independent spoiler and got Hillary reelected.

So, after Hillary was elected, there we were facing another four years of what they liked to call "fundamental transformation," and what we called "screwing up the country." I had never really thought about what I would do with my show after the election, so I just kept doing it even as I was halfheartedly being a lawyer. It took a while, but I built an audience and when the "pros" came to me it was with a pile of money because I had a built-in audience. Bye-bye legal career.

The mainstream media was dying, and we would laugh at its death throes, but it wasn't dead quite yet. We needed to help it along.

What we needed to do, as conservatives, was fight the very concept of a "mainstream media." The MSM [Mainstream Media] presupposed the gatekeeper function that it was desperately trying to preserve for itself. Gatekeepers have inordinate power; we conservatives needed to dissipate that power. To do that, we needed to get a wider variety of viewpoints out via the media.

In other words, we needed more conservative media targeted at everyday Americans—the ones for whom politics was not a 24/7 obsession.

There were three ways to do this. The first was actually the simplest: we would buy existing media platforms. Anyway, buying media took money. Of course, unless you are trying to buy *Newsweek*—remember that from the doctor's office as a kid? It got sold for about a dollar during the Obama years. Obviously, the vast majority of us weren't going to go buy a newspaper or a broadcast network, but a few rich guys could, and that was huge.

The second way was to infiltrate. Go in and be a part of the monster. Be like a virus—get in there and infest it and change it. That wasn't for me. I never wanted to be a journalist. I wanted to sound off! I wanted people to pay attention to me!

[*From the other room, Luke's voice booms, "Some things never change!" Chang furrows his brow, pets the terrier, which growls, and then continues.*]

181

The third way was the way most of us had to do it, and it was way, way tougher. We had to do it ourselves.

Technology made it possible. You could buy a mic, a video camera, and a laptop computer and you could have a show. There were these services that would transmit your shows over the Internet, and conservatives were suddenly up and making product. A lot was awful, but they kept at it. It was an incubator for conservative media talent. You would get these guys just making their Internet shows and pretty soon they would be on "real" radio. They would make their mistakes where no one saw them! Major players like Larry O'Connor, Derek Hunter, and Tony Katz got their start just like me, you know, just kind of putting on a show. Except it wasn't out in a barn—it was on the net.

And sometimes no one watched. I remember shows where I would have two guys in the chat room and one would be some leftist spewing homophobic crap. Leftists were the biggest homophobes I ever encountered—conservatives might not have liked thinking about my lifestyle, but they were always respectful. The leftists were just vulgar and gross.

Anyway, I learned. I learned how to set up and pace a show, how to handle calls, how to talk. It took me a long time, but by the time I got my first terrestrial radio hosting gig—a guest host job at a New Hampshire station—I had lost my "ums" and "uhhs." It was great training. When I got the call to come up to the big leagues, I was ready.

And I had a fan base. Conservatives were incredibly gracious and supportive. I guess we had to be, since the entire political establishment and media were against us. I had fans who listened in every day. Then they would promote me on social media through their Facebook and Twitter accounts—you need to understand how important those were to our organizing and communicating within the movement in the teens and twenties.

Yeah, they tried to shut us down. The resurrected Fairness Doctrine rule was just a transparent attempt to shut us up by trying to make sure we were weighted down with unlistenable liberal crap.

They called it "balance." I was conservative so I had to have "balance" to use the public airwaves. My stations freaked when Hillary's minions imposed the regulation; they were pretty much planning to switch to easy listening music until I came up with Chet the Fairness Guy.

Chet became my partner on the show. His favorite phrase was, "Duh, work is hard. Give me free money!" I would talk for a long while and then ask Chet the Fairness Guy if he had any insights and he'd usually say, "Duh, work is hard. Give me free money." This was our balance. It was a joke, and I treated it like that. Then the regulators came down on me and filed a complaint alleging that Chet the Fairness Guy was not "a legitimate representative of alternate political viewpoints."

Now, Chet was played by this guy name Neal Cornish who had a masters in political philosophy from Cornell and really knew his stuff. So when we sued, Neal goes up on the stand and articulates the liberal viewpoint perfectly to show he can, though he adds he doesn't believe a word of it because it's absolute nonsense. So the government then has to argue that the balance guy has to really believe in the alternate viewpoint he's expressing, and on appeal, even the liberal judges start getting uncomfortable at the idea that the government can go in and validate the sincerity and efficacy of every radio host in America.

Then I get up on the stand and start talking about what a mess the whole thing is, like if Chet the Fairness Guy and I agree

183

on something, did we have to go out and find someone else who didn't?

At the appellate argument, the government lawyers are getting furious because we are showing how stupid and fascist the whole thing was, and how unenforceable it would be even if the Constitution allowed it. They start arguing that if Chet the Fairness Guy won't make a good case for liberalism, then the government had a right to provide someone who would. The judges by then are just shaking their heads—except for one really leftist one, they were over it. The new Fairness Doctrine could not pass the straight face test and it got struck down. But every once in a while, Chet the Fairness Guy still comes to visit my show to rail about how much he hates the idea of work.

Colleen Hazlitt (Conservative Journalist)

We are walking through the New York Times reporter's "office," which is really no office at all but a corridor in the Cannon House Office Building on Capitol Hill. She never stops moving long enough to need a desk.

Our footsteps echo down the quiet halls of the aging building as we head toward the elevators. I struggle to keep up—the legendary reporter has to move fast to meet her deadlines. If I was not tagging along today, she'd be dictating her article into her iPhone 42 as she walks and letting the editing program proof and post it while she started her next project.

When I got here, these buildings were packed with people. Packed! Washington was the center of the universe. It was like a black hole, sucking in all the power and money from across the country. First with Obama, then with Clinton II, Washington was a boomtown. This was the place to be if you wanted influence, or if you were like me and wanted to write about people wielding influence.

I was conservative from a very young age. I never fell for liberalism, not in the least. I thought it was ridiculous and corrupt and I still do. But I also loved journalism. I had ever since I was a reporter on my middle school paper in the 2000s. I still do—the thrill of getting beneath the surface and getting the real story and then putting it out there . . . I love it.

I wanted to be on one of the biggest and best-known papers. I knew they were liberal fever swamps. Columbia Journalism School pretty much required you to swear fealty to the liberal creed. But I wanted to be part of that world, yet I wanted to be true to my beliefs. By the time I got to j-school, I wanted to promote conservatism through my journalism.

I was taught objectivity throughout my journalism education. They pounded it into us. But the fact is that "objectivity" in theory always meant liberalism in practice. Journalism education operated under the premise that we journalists were liberal and reinforced the idea that we were going to spend our careers supporting a liberal status quo. Most of my classmates, and later colleagues, were liberals, and they were happy and comfortable with their positions in the power structure. I wasn't, nor were the other conservatives I knew.

We wanted to shake things up, not only because conservatism was better policy-wise but because contrarian journalists would improve journalism as an institution. When I started in the second Obama term, and then when I got hired on at the *Washington Post* and eventually the *Times*, journalism was generally a low-quality product. Most journalists were trying desperately to cover for those in power while trying to hang onto their jobs in an industry most Americans had abandoned as irrelevant. If you know what the paper is always going to report—liberals good, conservatives bad—most people are going to get tired of it and go elsewhere for information.

So we wanted to save journalism, but to do that we had to change it. Changing journalism required that we conservatives infiltrate the media. Once we did that, we could change it from the inside. That's how guerrillas do it.

The media was overwhelmingly liberal in large part because the people going into the media were overwhelmingly liberal. Unlike in other fields that attract young, idealistic people—by which I mean unformed, immature people—there was no incentive to grow out of liberalism over time. Say you went into business as a 24-year-old liberal. By the time you are 30, you're probably thinking Milton Friedman was a squish. Experience and accountability spur maturation.

But if you went into journalism as a 24-year-old liberal, six years later you are a slightly balder, slightly fatter liberal with the mentality of a 24-year-old. There was no accountability, no hard knocks, other than the changes in the industry itself. You would tell yourself that those changes were not *your* fault—your audience just was not wise enough to appreciate your work. And there was a newsroom full of other liberals reinforcing all the stupid things your college professors taught you.

As a journalist, you wanted to see yourself as some kind of white knight fighting for truth and justice where, in reality, you were usually just a hack. A teacher often teaches because he can't do, but at least he *teaches*. Journalists did not even do that much. They just *talked* about stuff—and then drank cheap, happy hour Bud Light and told each other how awesome they were.

A whole generation of liberals became reporters because of

Woodward and Bernstein and *All the President's Men*, a turning point in journalism that gave them the terrible idea that they were not just there to chronicle what was happening but to put their fingers on the scale to ensure the *right* thing happens. Of course, the right thing was always the left thing.

But there is something honorable and important about journalism in a free country, just not the hackneyed propaganda version of journalism we had been treated to since the 1960s. The media was barely even pretending anymore, which hastened the decline that new technology made a foregone conclusion.

If you are going to get force-fed ideology anyway, why would you ever choose to listen to someone who denies he has one even as he forces it down your throat? The scant audiences for the network newscasts were grim testimony to the failure of the "journalist as hidden advocate" model. It was bad enough watching the endless series of commercials about Cialis and diabetes testers without having the network anchors lie to your face.

It was clear that the new media world would shake out, and if we wanted to be part of it, we conservatives needed to show up. So I did, and so did others. We started showing up. There were more and more conservative journalists every day. While I went the traditional route—and got a solid background in the mechanics of journalism and reporting by doing so—most of them were learning their craft online either working for themselves or for some of the bigger sites. This was a huge talent pool, and one where the journalists themselves had a following.

The question was how long the struggling mainstream media outlets could ignore them? They tried—they would hire liberals off the web, but shunned conservatives until some were just too popular to ignore. Many never did decide to hire conservatives—they would rather go bankrupt than go an inch to the right, but other outlets that wanted to survive started scooping these folks up.

With conservative journalists who had no incentive to cover for the liberal establishment coming in, particularly during the Clinton administration, we started seeing something like investigative journalism again. That was a dying art in the Obama/Clinton years. It should be no surprise why—government was expanding and gathering more power and control over peoples' everyday lives, and liberal journalists generally supported this. They had no incentive to reveal government's failures and every incentive to cover them up.

Which they did, shamelessly, causing great damage to the credibility of journalism as a whole. The American people saw journalists as simply another kind of hack, looking them in the eyes and lying to them. Not surprising, no one outside of the newsrooms was mourning when newspaper and after newspaper closed and magazine after magazine got sold off for a buck.

Journalism had to change or die, and the most important people to the cause of changing journalism, beyond the lateral hires from established websites, were the true infiltrators. People like me. In the past, conservatives had seemed to self-select away from the media into more friendly realms like business and other fields that conservatives believed actually produce value for humanity. I disagreed. I always thought that journalism—true journalism that afflicts the comfortable and comforts the afflicted—is hugely important in a democratic republic. The hallelujah chorus of leftist journalists was not just an embarrassment to the profession but a danger to democracy.

So, we needed young conservatives to change the paradigm and start looking at journalism, a career they might not have otherwise considered. But we had to be sneaky about it. It was very covert.

I would get a sense about new hires, get to know them a bit, make sure they were sympathetic, and then dramatically reveal my conservatism to them. They were usually relieved to have another weirdo right-winger in the newsroom. They were no longer alone.

I weaseled myself onto the team that went out to college campuses to hire at career fairs. If I determined a candidate was conservative, I would be very clear: "Hide your conservatism! Keep your free market light under a basket! Let them keep thinking you are another brain-dead college grad who actually believes that stuff about America being racist, imperialist, sexist, homophobic and . . . uh . . . racist!" The word "racist" was always huge back then.

I would tell them, "Smile when the weary hacks who have infested the newsroom for a couple decades spew their liberal silliness. They'll be laid off soon anyway. Bide your time." And as they bided their time, they started subtly changing the dynamic.

For me, it began with some tiny rebellions. This Republican congressman got picked up at a brothel in Washington partying with a bunch of football players from the Washington Redskins. Now, when some Republican half-wit did something stupid, we were sure to mention his party prominently. I put it in the second paragraph—I didn't think about it. It just seemed to fit there in the flow of the story. But I also added some detail on the last Democrat busted with hookers in the city a couple months before. Two in a couple months—I saw it as a trend and therefore relevant.

Oh boy, was there a reaction. My editor moved the Republican reference to the first sentence, which was fair enough. But he cut out the part about the Democrat's arrest, telling me it was not important to the story. Frankly, I thought "DC's Hooker-Happy Politicians" would have made for a great investigative series, but I'm pretty sure that would have removed my editor from most of the best guest lists so it was never going to happen.

Oh, and my editor refused to let me call the team the "Redskins"—it was racist, you see—and he added some text about the team name controversy implying that the congressman was insensitive to Native Americans because the people he chose to cavort with in the house of ill repute were members of a team with an offensive name.

So, the next month a Democratic congressman got caught in a Baltimore bus station sodomy sting. I wrote it up and, having learned my lesson, mentioned that he was a Democrat right in the first paragraph. Heck, *he* thought being a Democrat was important—he had spoken at the last Democratic convention the previous year about how the GOP did not have a monopoly on family values. I put that part in too and submitted it. My editor flipped. "What are you trying to do?" he asked me. "This will kill his career!"

I kept up my personal campaign of clarity and truth. I did tiny things, like letting people know when a scumbag *wasn't* a Republican—because if he was a Republican scumbag the media ensured everyone knew he was a Republican. Telling the whole truth became a powerful act of rebellion.

Once we got a foothold and started restoring basic journalistic standards, we would ask hard questions of—get this, because it seemed wacky at the time—politicians of *both* parties. When you might ask a Republican, "Well, Senator Miser, wouldn't the programs you propose cutting hurt the people who count on them to survive," maybe you then ask the Democrat,

"So, Senator Handout, why should people who actually work for a living have their tax money taken and given to people who refuse to?"

Of course, this caused a furor in the newsroom. But now we were pushing back. We would say, "Look, this is great because Senator Handout will probably vapor lock and have to be carried off to a mental hospital. That's news! People want to see what happens when it gets real for politicians." It was crazy—we had to argue in favor of actual journalism. When our editors would have heartburn, we would look innocent and say, "Well, don't you want me to ask tough questions?" Then we'd add, "I'm just speaking truth to power."

Of course, it also helped our agenda. Not only would the readers get a point of view the mainstream media tried to ensure they had never had before, but when that liberal freaked out it would leave an opening for a Republican governor to fill.

The media then was a powerful weapon for progressives, but it was in decline as printed newspapers faded to cocktail napkin size and the nightly news became the realm of sexually dysfunctional old people pining for FDR. The new media arose, and mainstream journalism had to adapt. It is less objective today—or, rather, it pretends it is objective less—and much more decentralized.

The old mainstream media is a thing of the past. Big, proud institutions like the *New York Times* and ABC and the like evolved into online content providers, albeit ones with better name recognition at the beginning. We have had to work to keep our audience at the *Times*—we cannot take it for granted, which is why I am here on Capitol Hill every day, talking to people, touching base with sources, getting real news the only way you can—by real reporting.

Do I miss objectivity? I never knew objectivity. All I ever saw was a liberal echo chamber, and I figured if that was how it was going to be, then I wanted our story to be the one that was echoing. Look, I am a reporter, not a propagandist. If all I ever do is praise the Republicans and trash the Democrats, I'm going to have terrific sources among the GOP and none among the Dems. Both sides know I will give them a fair shake—I won't give either side a break, but I will make sure their side gets told even if I have to report other facts that show their side is a crock.

I think my views against "objectivity" as a concept—which even today are controversial among journalists—are really a reaction to what I experienced coming up in the Obama and Clinton years. Whenever anyone starts talking about "objectivity," I immediately flash back to years and years when objectivity was just another way of saying, "Support and reinforce the liberal status quo." I don't think objectivity exists. I've never seen it truly practiced. I think I can function best by making my views known and dealing with people honestly and fairly.

I think the media today is much better. It's much more conservative-friendly than it was, but we did not hesitate to reveal the corruption scandals in the last couple Republican administrations. I voted for Carrie Marlowe, but when her Secretary of Energy got caught selling off assets as she was closing down the Department of Energy, I didn't hesitate to run it on the front page.

I am a conservative—I don't cover for government failures. That's the opposite of what I believe! In fact, I infuriated a j-school panel a few years ago when I told the audience that a liberal political reporter has a built-in conflict of interest because he loves the idea of the government he is supposed to ruthlessly show is failing. I have not been asked back!

We succeeded in changing things, though. As conservatives, we needed to be in the game. We needed to show up. We could no longer cede the critical node of news and information to a coterie of leftists with zero compunction about turning it into a 24/7 propaganda tool for whatever leftist was in power or aspiring to it.

We conservatives needed to become part of the media, and we did. We did it by making ourselves invaluable. To break in, we had to encourage young conservatives to hide their views just enough to get inside the fortress. We were Trojan horses. And once inside, while the liberals were asleep, we crept downstairs to unlock the front gate.

Paul Warner (News Anchor)

"Sometimes I wish I could be Walter Cronkite," admits Paul Warner, the new anchor for the NewsRight network's evening news show *Right Update*. With an average rating of 5.4, it is among the highest rated of all the evening news and political shows, even though it counts as viewers about only 1 in 20 Americans.

Cronkite would have something like one in three TVs in America watching him every night 75 years ago. He had a lot of power, but he had to pretend to be objective although it was pretty clear he was very much a man of the left. Now, I can be open with my biases because I don't presume to speak as some gatekeeper of acceptable ideas. You can find any ideas that interest you out there! If you come to NewsRight, you'll get news from a constitutional conservative perspective with no apologies.

I started with NewsRight in 2017. It used to be MSNBC, but they were doing poorly and a bunch of wealthy conservatives bought it. Let's just say the day they revealed who the buyers were caused some consternation in the headquarters! The rest of the media was apoplectic, almost as much as when conservatives bought the old *Los Angeles Times.*

We were a direct competitor to the Fox News Channel from the right. Fox had come in as a conservative alternative, but it still tried to be part of the objective paradigm. It really was fair and balanced (that was actually its motto) because it would actually acknowledge conservative ideas and concerns. I loved Fox, and it was critical to keeping conservatism alive during the Obama days and it remains a powerhouse today.

But we were different. We were outright advocates for constitutional conservative values, where most other outfits claimed to be objective. Getting more conservatives into newsrooms and on television and on the web news shows that still embraced the objective model had a huge effect. It was not so much the on-air presentation—that was the last to start changing away from liberal bias—but the choice of stories and the production and editing.

You'd have these very liberal anchors and you could see them biting their lips as they had to read news copy and introduce clips that just totally undercut the liberal narrative. I remember one almost fainting over a story about a welfare cheat who was bragging on air about having five kids from five different fathers to get all sorts of government handouts. You would have never seen that in the past, though it was absolutely true and absolutely a story. But that anchor had no choice but to grit his teeth and read a story that probably converted a few thousand citizens away from liberalism!

194 Competition was only a part of it. The other key component was conservatives working their way up on the inside. For years,

conservatives had stayed out of journalism, but the web and guys like Andrew Breitbart inspired talented conservatives to go out and get jobs in the media as journalists.

It could be hard to get a job, and hard to keep one, if you were a known conservative. I remember one reporter at ABC was found to be conservative and fired. Well, he sued under the new federal Political Discrimination Act that made it illegal to fire someone over their political beliefs if the job was not expressly political. Well, ABC had to argue that being an "objective" reporter was political, and that really hurt their credibility.

Oh, as a conservative I thought the law was inappropriate— it's none of the government's business why you choose to hire or not hire someone—but after Obama and Hillary we got a lot less fussy about using liberals' own tactics against them! It's our media now.

10

BREAKING AND REMAKING THE LAW

"When Everything Is a Crime, Everyone Is a Criminal"

Conservatives had long defended a criminal justice system that dispensed little justice and was barely even a system. But by the 2010s it was obvious that the system was failing—and as the liberal administrations abused the justice system for their short-term political ends, it became clear that it required conservative attention. By embracing conservative values, the insurgency drew new recruits while leaving the liberals to defend a decaying, discredited institution.

■ ■ ■

Jerome Timms (Republican Congressman)

The conservatives first brought up eliminating the mandatory minimum sentences and vastly cutting back the drug war when they only had the House. The liberals thought this was great—and they immediately got to the conservatives' right on it, calling them soft on crime and so forth. But no one bought that—the conservatives were plenty tough. They just wanted to be smart about the problem, and more important, fair.

It was black urban Democrats who joined the Republicans to pass the bill. Hillary vetoed it—she said, "Someone has to protect the village's children." By then my mom was in jail and I was a teenager. I was disgusted. Hillary knew better than us what was good for us? I understood then how sometimes racists smile at you like they're your friends. And how sometimes the people other people tell you are racist aren't.

I started working as an aide in Congress on the big Criminal Review Project. We went through every federal law, statute, and regulation and recommended changes to reduce penalties, make them clearer, or get rid of them entirely. When we started, the experts told us the average American was inadvertently committing three felonies a day. That's unacceptable in a free country.

There were just too damn many laws, too damn many rules, and too damn many crimes. When everything is a crime, everyone is a criminal. And everyone is then at the mercy of the government.

Prosecutors had too damn much discretion, and far too many people were getting caught up in the criminal justice system. Ending that un-American state of affairs was the right thing to do, and for Republicans, it was a politically smart thing to do.

It was not just about drug laws, though drug laws presented a huge target for politically savvy reform. Look at me—my mother's release from prison was because of it, and reform won Republicans a lot of credibility.

It was also intellectual property law where huge corporate interests turned civil infractions into criminal offenses. It was

computer laws where simply breaching a contract was a crime—
a crime, punishable by jail! Did that protect society? No, it was
not just a waste of judicial resources but it put the government
in the role of enforcer for companies who, if they wanted their
intellectual property protected, should have hired lawyers to go
do it.

What do you call a system that made it a crime to "jailbreak"
your iPhone? We conservatives called it ridiculous. But it used
to be a reality.

The liberals, aided and abetted by some Republicans, had created a system that criminalized conduct that should not, under
any reasonable, rational, or just conception, be considered criminal—civil maybe, but in a lawsuit you only seek money. Here,
they would throw you in jail.

I remember one kid, a genius in Boston, got indicted for going
into a computer system. He didn't damage anything. Sure, what
he did was wrong, but he was looking at years in jail—years of
his life! He killed himself. That's not just crazy—it's unjust.

Think about it—thanks to a craven Congress doing the bid-
ding of a bunch of giant companies, you could be labeled a felon
and put in prison—at our expense, mind you—for *years* for the
"crime" of displeasing some conglomerate.

Moreover, when you combined these unjust laws with the
nearly unfettered discretion of prosecutors, you had a justice
system that was functionally indistinguishable from an *in*justice
system.

The goal of prosecutors stopped being to seek justice—it was
to get convictions. Part of that was our fault collectively. Reacting to the shameful mugger-hugger liberalism of the past, we
encouraged a crackdown on criminals. Fair enough, but then
when crime stopped being such a concern, we turned away and

199

the prosecutors, acting in our names, kept it up without accountability. You could hardly blame them—it was up to us as citizens to ask not just how many convictions they got, but were they *just* results?

Well, we constitutional conservatives started doing that. A lot of religious folks were very focused on reforming the justice system, and so were libertarians. Then you added the minority community that felt itself victimized and you had the ultimate strange bedfellow coalition.

Criminal justice system reform was a twofer for constitutional conservatives—it was the right thing to do, and it was a powerful wedge aimed right at the heart of the liberal coalition because it split out minorities and the young.

When everything was a crime and liberals chose who got prosecuted (people like us) and who didn't (other liberals—did you see any arrests after the 2008 Wall Street scandals?), it gave them tremendous power.

We thought, "Let's take it away from them, and in the process show young people and minorities why conservatism is their friend." The liberals walked right into the trap. They couldn't help but resist because every reform we proposed would strip them of power.

When we took power again, we started reigning in the "fourth branch" of government—bureaucracy—by reasserting Congress's proper role as creators of laws rather than delegators. We tried to withdraw from the various agencies the power to "interpret" law through regulations in such a way as to create criminal conduct. We felt that the federal government had no business criminalizing behavior without a vote by the Congress and the signature of the president on the entirety of the law. Elected representatives had to personally vote on—and be accountable for—each infraction that could support criminal liability.

When the liberals started whining, we threw the idea of fining some little kid for helping an injured bird back in their faces.

We pushed to require that every criminal law have an intent element—no more strict liability violations where the government need not prove the specific intent to commit the alleged "crime." When the libs whined about this—they really thought this was a great issue to base their comeback on—we would give the examples of people ruined because some chemical spilled on their land and they didn't even know it, but were prosecuted anyway because intent wasn't an element of the crime. President Marlowe was totally behind us.

While the Democrats were busy protecting their ability to inflict injustices on innocent Americans, we hit them again, this time with a real nuke. Prosecutors used to be able to load up dozens of charges for the same thing against an accused. These are called "counts." With so many counts, there would be the potential for enormous sentences, essentially forcing the accused to plea bargain out or risk decades in jail if he demanded his right to trial. It was designed to encourage plea bargaining, but it caught up innocent people because they couldn't risk demanding a trial. Sure, sometimes lots of charges are justified—there are bad people out there—but the risk to innocent folks was far too great. It was just wrong, and we stopped it.

We used a four-pronged approach to solve other problems with the system.

First, our reforms allowed the defendant to put exonerating evidence before the grand jury. Indictments used to be handed down after the grand jury heard only from the prosecutor. We empowered citizens once again to truly decide who gets prosecuted and who doesn't.

They used to say a prosecutor could get a grand jury to indict a ham sandwich. That's a disgrace—we directed grand juries to be informed that their most important duty was *not* to indict if the prosecutor did not meet his burden. That changed the whole focus of the system, from assembly line into an individualized process designed to protect the innocent.

Second, we took more power from the prosecutor and gave it back to grand juries. For any case where the potential sentence exceeds five years, we now allow the grand jury to propose a plea bargain, and if the prosecutor doesn't wish to offer it, the judge may direct that it be offered.

Third, we required that the US attorneys reveal plea bargain offers to juries—they may wonder, rightly, why the US attorney would have accepted five years before trial but is asking for 30 years because the citizen demanded his right to a trial. The prosecutors were furious, but if the government can't stand behind its actions, then we have a problem.

And fourth, our reforms required the federal government to pay the reasonable costs of defense for those charges it could not prove to a jury. That took care of a lot of the shakiest charges we used to see on those 100-count Christmas tree indictments, which is good. A prosecutor should not bring any charges he does not believe he can prove beyond a reasonable doubt anyway. Moreover, too many lives were being ruined and too many innocent people left destitute by having to fight dozens of false criminal charges. A jury sees a hundred-count indictment and figures, "Gee, something here has to be true," even if it isn't.

What did the Democrats do? They tried to get to our right on crime, and we were happy to let them. That left us minorities, libertarians, and young people, as well as constitutional conservatives.

The justice system still isn't perfect today, but it's no longer a disgrace. We promised to fix it and we did. And in the process, we helped to win over folks who used to blame *us* for this kind of injustice.

We wanted to win over the young, tech-savvy, 20-something generation, so we decided to not be the side that wanted to stick them in a federal prison for a third of a century for a glorified violation of a computer terms of service advisory.

We ended the so-called War on Drugs. I detest drugs and get tired of users, but I also detested cops getting killed saving people from themselves. And I hate the human and fiscal cost of putting admittedly stupid, often not great people in jail for decades over pharmaceuticals. I experienced that damage firsthand.

After Marlowe's pardons, we pushed to reevaluate drug sentences, not because we like drug users but because the old approach was not solving the problem and was causing more problems than it solved. Putting people in jail for decades was clearly not deterring the conduct—if doing what we were doing worked, we'd have been a drug-free paradise of hard-working, solid citizens.

Note that we also pushed through a ban on any federal government aid for drug users. If the states want to subsidize them, fine, but as far as the federal government goes, if you use drugs you are on your own.

We needed to relook at our strategy not for the benefit of the people who got prosecuted but for our own benefit. Imprisoning people should be a last resort—though there are plenty of knuckleheads whose behavior puts them far beyond the last resort. We need to save jail for people who should be in jail.

The minority community viewed the drug war as an assault upon itself. Moreover, because it was the police who enforced the drug war—and because police are about the only "conservative" government workers—we conservatives ended up getting the blame for all the abuses and negative consequences.

Many minority Democrats saw what we were trying to do, and they were natural allies with conservatives for pro-family, pro-community justice system reform designed to minimize the impact of drugs while preserving families and strengthening communities. To their credit, they rejected the Clinton administration's pleas not to cooperate with us.

The inner cities are still the least conservative parts of this country, not counting faculty lounges, and are therefore most in need of conservative solutions. We needed to be in these communities, if not winning them then at least making the liberals break a sweat to retain them. Criminal justice reform was just the ticket to earn us a fresh look

There were just too many damn laws. I think there still are. The federal government, frankly, has almost no business criminalizing any more behavior. Crime is predominately a state problem. Every new law is, therefore, an expansion of government, which is presumptively bad. Instead of coming up with a hundred new laws a year, we tried to change the dynamic to come up with a hundred to repeal. Or, better yet, two hundred.

Law is a powerful weapon in the hands of a too-powerful government. We started stripping some of that power away, and we did it in the name of the values of fairness, compassion, and justice. You know, the stuff liberals lie about holding dear.

Billy Coleman (Activist)

Coleman's raw milk farming is what had originally brought him into conflict with Walmart and other large companies that had used their connections to drive small competitors under. As a liberal, what he did not expect was to see the full weight of the criminal justice system fall upon him.

In the late 2010s, I was running an organic farm. No antibiotics, not hormones, no chemicals—nothing. Pure cow. That was our motto: "Jacob's Creek Farms: Pure Cow."

Well, we sold in little stores around the region. A lot of these stores were mom and pop operations. I knew a bunch were Tea Partiers, and I didn't like that because at the time I was what you would probably call a liberal. But, you know, they did their thing and I did mine. They wanted to sell my milk and I wanted them to, so we were cool.

Well, they start going under because Walmart was undercutting them. Then all sorts of new regulations come on that most of these small stores couldn't handle. The Walmarts and the other big companies didn't even notice the new regulations—in fact, they had supported them. It crushed the little guys!

What was keeping these small stores going was partly that they would sell raw milk. People would drive out from the city to buy it. Well, sure enough the feds start coming around, telling us our local raw milk is unsafe and we can't sell it. The hell with that—my milk was healthier than any of that processed junk that Walmart was selling. Of course, Walmart was all over the campaign to ban local raw milk. They said it was to protect the children. We said it was to protect their profits.

Well, we keep selling our stuff and we start getting harassed. One day, I am out in the barn and suddenly I am looking down the barrels of a bunch of assault rifles!

I thought they had made some kind of mistake, but they hadn't. They came to serve a search warrant on my farm and they brought the SWAT team. Why the hell did the Agriculture Department have a SWAT team anyway?

I got charged with a bunch of violations, including conspiracy. I was looking at 10 years in federal prison and losing my farm. They offered me a plea deal—plea to a felony, do two years, but I still lose my farm because it is "a mechanism of a criminal enterprise." My lawyer told me to take it, but I told the deputy US attorney to go to hell.

I thought I was done for, but then I started getting all this support from these conservatives, and not just in my area. I started getting interviewed on conservative media—the regular media ignored it—and I got so well-known that the US attorney tried to revoke my bail.

The feds complained to the judge that the conservatives were trying to taint the jury pool. They sure as shit were. The jury heard the evidence, saw that I was guilty as hell of selling raw milk, and acquitted me.

The feds went ballistic. There were more raw milk prosecutions and more acquittals. The feds finally got a judge to issue a gag order saying that no one could discuss the raw milk cases in public because it "perverted justice." Well, there was sure some justice being perverted all right, but not by us.

The juries were still refusing to convict—it was called "jury nullification," and juries were doing it on gun cases too after Hillary Clinton put her ban in effect. Finally, liberal judges started *ordering* juries to convict, and when they wouldn't, the judges would just find the accused guilty themselves. The Supreme Court even upheld that travesty until the impeachments and President Marlowe's pardons.

Now, I sell raw milk to anyone who wants to buy it. I figure if you are an adult, you can decide for yourself what you put into your body. The government has no business being involved.

I had been a liberal, but after I got to really know liberalism, well, count me out.

Puff (Hemp Advocate and Activist)

Puff is clearly feeling it now. He inhales deeply once more before continuing.

You know, I'm just doing my thing. I wasn't hurting anyone. But they were putting people in jail for years, making it dangerous to buy. Why? The constitutional conservatives supported decriminalization, so I was with them.

After all, you can't get more constitutional than weed. I mean, they all grew hemp. Madison, Jefferson, Lincoln, all those guys. George Washington's wig? Made of hemp. I'm serious—weed's as American as apple pie!

Brad Fields (Insurance Salesman)

Sure, I fired up a fattie or two in school. Everyone did. And if letting the stoners get stoned—which they were doing already—was all it took to get a bunch of libertarians fighting beside us for the freedoms the liberals wanted to take, I was like, "Go ahead and inhale!"

207

Tamara Hayes Smith (Professor/Activist)

It was tough. There is always a tension between the pragmatic and the principled, but at a certain point the choice becomes whether or not a given hill is worth dying on. Conservatives faced the question of whether making sure pot smokers couldn't legally buy the pot that they were already buying was worth risking the entire republic. And the answer was no.

11

TARGET ACADEMIA

"Nothing Is More Conservative Than a Liberal Faculty"

Academia was key high ground for the insurgency. Not only did it have enormous prestige that progressives could harness to gain support for their plans, but it provided progressives a perfect venue for indoctrination. The constitutional conservatives found it an irresistible target as their power—and academia's arrogance—grew.

■ ■ ■

David Chang (Conservative Media Host)

The controversial Chang makes it a point to mention his Ivy League credentials not so much for the sake of vanity but because it emphasizes his rejection of the values and beliefs his professors tried to inculcate in him. "I came from the belly of the beast," he says. "I experienced the best they had and rejected it."

On his shows, particularly in the early years, academic antics were a staple of his commentary. "The universities are supposed to preserve and defend our culture, and I was appalled by what they chose to preserve and defend."

You could always count on filling a couple hours a week with the progressive nonsense at some college somewhere. They thought they were safe in their little academic bubble, and that no one would know what they were doing. Wrong!

I loved to shine a spotlight on them and catch them in the act enforcing some idiotic feminist speech code or having some sort of weird sex festival for freshmen. But what started happening is that normal people began wondering why they were getting taxed for this kind of crap—much less paying six figures for their kids to go to a traditional university, when they could get a real education via the web for a fraction of the price with no nonsense.

As constitutional conservatives, we began to realize that the entire higher education system was a giant scam designed to take money from people who contribute to society and transfer it to layabout academics and their enablers while simultaneously indoctrinating our young people in the precepts of collectivism. And in the Obama years, there was a "higher education bubble"—a law professor named Glenn Reynolds, who had a very popular site called *Instapundit*, coined that term. Well, by the 2010s, the bubble was already popping.

We started to identify academia, as it was then structured, as what it was—an enemy. Then we needed to move swiftly and mercilessly to assist the natural processes of the market in changing it into something that would not only be useful to society again but that was no longer a subsidized petri dish for the virus of progressivism.

The higher education scam—well, it was technically more of a racket—was actually kind of brilliant in a sinister way. The higher education establishment built its success on two pillars, both of which have crumbled over the last 30 years.

The first was the ridiculous notion that everyone could and should go to college. No, everyone couldn't and everyone shouldn't. Most people shouldn't go to college, at least as it was commonly understood back then. Then, it was a four- to six-year time-out from life, with giant lecture hall classes and not much in the way of relevant learning, all for incredible amounts of money. And the focus was on having had the experience—of walking out with the diploma—rather than actual learning. Some schools even gave up on grades—it was simply enough to have been accepted as a high schooler. Four years later you got a piece of paper and no one checked or cared whether you actually learned anything.

If we had had a K-12 educational system whose purpose was to educate kids to a decent level instead of to provide jobs for teachers and administrative parasites, most people would have walked out of high school with the kind of core competency required to be a valuable citizen. As it was then, many of our "colleges" were devoted to teaching students the things they should have learned in high school.

We did not have "higher" education; we mostly just had "longer" education.

The false notion that everyone should go to college created an artificial need for colleges. Look at the vast array of so-called colleges that was out there then, including community colleges. We had to face facts—most students at these institutions didn't need any more school. They needed to get their asses to work.

211

So, you got young people who weren't really focused on—or good at—academic work taking valuable time out of their lives to struggle through basic courses that added zero value to their marketability. Worse, they were taking on debt to do it. And staying in school longer meant delaying adulthood—that and marriage penalties in law helped lead to extended adolescent periods that we had never seen before in our society.

We finally just cut the baloney about expanding minds and growing as individuals and all that crap—the college scam was a full employment program for a liberal educator class who made their living pretending to educate students who, in return, pretended to learn.

The so-called prestige institutions were little better, dominated by phony majors and nonsense courses, with ever-dropping standards that ensured that something like half the students had an "A" average if their school bothered giving grades at all.

People—parents paying the bills, employers hiring these grads, and even the students themselves—started realizing that when everyone is outstanding, no one is.

This whole apparatus was funded by the government through student loans that could either never be repaid or anchored the graduates (assuming they ever graduated, which a high proportion did not) in debt for decades. And for what? At the crappy schools, the diplomas meant nothing, and at the good ones, they were usually just a souvenir of a four-year vacation full of cheap beer and cheesy sexual experimentation—with a $350,000 price tag.

This couldn't go on and it didn't. The cost to support this bloated pyramid scheme was rising too fast while the peasants were revolting at the sticker shock. College just cost too much, and people began to realize that they simply were not getting value for the money. Further, technology was making the old model of having some tenured jerk droning on to an auditorium of hungover sophomores a thing of the past. Why spend hundreds of thousands of dollars to live in residence at Deadend State when you could go online and get a Science 101 lecture from a Nobel Prize winner for free?

In the end, it was pretty clear that the real product these schools were selling was a diploma. When the high-prestige schools figured out how to credential students online, and that became widely accepted, it was adios academia as we knew it. The low-end schools just couldn't compete, and the high-end ones had to change to meet the realities of cost and new technology. The traditional university model of a few decades ago is a specialty model now—most college courses are online and 90 percent of students are nonresidents, living real lives and fitting in education around careers.

Politically, academia was a festering boil of progressivism that had to be lanced. We were always focused on the culture, and academia was a huge component of that. Protected from accountability by tenure and the unearned prestige of their positions, academics turned the "best" schools in the country into training grounds for little liberal fascists, ruthlessly enforcing their own creepy little police states of politically correct oppression. Nothing is more conservative than a liberal faculty, and they tried to resist but their old model of a university was dying.

It was time to kick them when they were down.

First, conservatives fought the idea that every kid needs to go to college. This was a very tough sell with the middle class, particularly because they had been used to seeing a university education as a ticket upwards for their children. But now they were seeing the opposite with their own eyes—their kids were

213

coming home with their bags and a diploma, smothered in debt, unable to find decent work in the Obama/Clinton economy.

With money tight and prices astronomical, parents were a bit more open to the idea that their kid might be better off being a plumber instead of getting a degree in contemporary feminist theater and fixing artisanal coffee drinks for the rest of his life.

Conservatives supported trade schools in high schools—if you were a certified electric vehicle technician, you couldn't *not* get a job. Now, this ran up against the teachers unions and the campaigns to centralize education standards like the failed Common Core program Obama and a bunch of squishy Republicans tried to foist on the country during the teens. This old guard wanted to retain the old, failed model—too many Democratic constituents in the teachers unions were too invested in it to let there be reform without a fight.

It was in the red states where constitutional conservative governors and legislators started making the real changes. Of course, the biggest and most important change was outlawing public employee unions. When the teachers unions started to go away, then the biggest obstacle to real education reform was gone.

We backed other key reforms too. At the university level, we first started linking student loans to majors, at least until we could eliminate government loans and grants entirely.

If you wanted to be a physics major, sure, here was your loan at 5 percent. There was a place for physics majors in society. But if you wanted to major in the ethnomusicology of Angola? Awesome. Live your dream. The interest rate was 12 percent because, well, your dream was stupid and there was no good reason the rest of us should pay a dime to help you achieve it.

Interested in majoring in sociology? I think we charged 22 percent! It was even more useless. The same with any kind of racial, ethnic, gender, or sexual preference "studies." Those idiotic, pseudomajors actually made America a worse place. The academics, of course, went nuts. It was delightful. And no loans for law school. We had too damn many lawyers already.

Of course, the variable student loan rates were only an interim step. The Constitution says nothing about subsidizing people's higher education, and the program was simply a stealth subsidy for a Democratic constituency anyway. We ended the government student loan program completely in 2030, and while fewer people graduate from college today, employers have responded by not demanding a degree where the position really doesn't require one.

Oh, there are still private student loans you can get from private companies, but they are not government subsidized or government backed. And they are not exempt from being discharged in bankruptcy. That's why lenders are very careful about their loans these day.

The sell got easier over time as people changed their views about higher education. We asked, "Why should we subsidize nonsense?" We let the Democrats explain why some mom working 50 hours a week then having to take care of her kids should pay taxes to let some jerk get a performance art degree from Princeton.

Sure, there were some real majors, and science training was and is important, but those weren't the issue and those weren't the problem. We all knew the problem because we all saw it when we went to school. The academic elite was unaccountable, untouchable, and always greedy for more.

215

We conservatives decided to crush it.

We hit them in the pocketbook, where it hurt. Some of the institutions had ungodly amounts of cash squirreled away, like my own alma mater Harvard, yet they let Uncle Sucker keep picking up the tab. We started requiring them to pay out a minimum of 10 percent of their endowment annually to be eligible for any federal aid of any kind and to remain tax-free. You would have thought we were killing puppies on the library steps!

Our goal? Shrink the liberal industrial complex by getting rid of marginal, bogus schools that served no purpose other than to employ its left-wing employees. This made sense fiscally, policy-wise, and it supported our effort to eliminate progressivism as a viable alternative to conservatism.

Oh, let's be clear. Hastening the destruction of academia as it used to be was not just about education policy. We learned from liberals—destroy your enemies by doing whatever it took. Academia was perhaps the most solid base of progressivism in the culture. Academia had ruthlessly purged any conservative elements from its ranks. We needed to be just as ruthless. A bunch of otherwise marginally employable losers, called "academics," somehow managed to get themselves permanent gigs at society's expense and use it as a base to wreck society. We needed to go after them.

In the states we controlled, we eliminated tenure—just ended it outright. We called it what it was—an accountability measure. Later, at the federal level, we linked interim student loan funding to "tenure reform." If you wanted your professors untouchable, you didn't get to touch our money. The universities folded.

But even as we helped the market break up academia, we attacked their reign of campus terror. We were especially effective at the state level where we controlled the legislatures.

We strengthened discrimination laws to expressly cover political viewpoints, and then we helped conservatives shut out of academia to sue. There was nothing that got the attention of an administrator like getting served with a lawsuit. It was all progressive fun and games until someone was handed a subpoena to a deposition to explain why there were 58 Democrats in the English Department and zero Republicans. Boy, it was fun watching them try to explain that.

We pushed free speech laws that barred the academic fascists from harassing and silencing people simply for expressing their conservative beliefs. We made the liberals show that they were the party of repression and censorship by opposing these commonsense reforms.

Oh, and we mandated equal funding for student organizations. When I was in school, it was a constant battle for our conservative paper to get funded, though the Marxist ones (including ones run by nonstudents!) always got a boatload of cash. And we got conservative rich guys to throw a few bucks at some underemployed young conservative lawyers to fund the cases.

Administrators would always, always do the easiest thing. The easiest thing had been buckling under to the faculty fascists. But when we got some lawyers involved, we would watch those administrators get super-duper concerned about things like free speech, nondiscrimination, and due process.

There is still a place for academia in America, of course. Except today it is a smaller place for fewer people, but with much more rigorous standards and a true dedication to knowledge and free inquiry. Yesterday, it was a racket and a joke, and it was ruining young lives with debt incurred earning useless degrees in silly subjects. Today it adds value to society—and conservatives are free to participate in it again.

217

Academia made us its enemy. We had no second thoughts when we helped the market ruthlessly reform it. Academia as we knew it was doomed anyway by economics and technology. We constitutional conservatives simply helped hasten its death and rebirth.

And we smiled as we did.

Ted Jindal (Technology Consultant)

As a UC Berkeley graduate (class of 2010), Jindal certainly has impressive academic credentials. However, even though he is the owner of a multimillion-dollar technology company, he is critical of the academic world that he came from.

My computer science degree was useful to me. It helped me do my actual work—you can't say that about people like my roommate in the dorms. He was a sociology major, and last I heard he was a waiter at a steakhouse in Long Beach.

Technology changed the nature of college. These professors had been teaching the same way for centuries; then suddenly their whole world was turned upside down. What was the advantage of sitting in a giant hall with 500 other sophomores to hear some famous professor if you could do it in your house, at a time you chose, for a hundredth the cost—and rewind it if you missed something? Suddenly, these academic superstores became totally fungible.

Technology was going to force change regardless, but the arrogance of academia took away any incentive to provide them a soft landing. The old university model made its bed, and it died in it.

Delbert Windbridge (Liberal Professor)

Professor Windbridge of Duke University has the reputation of being an unhappy man. A staunch liberal, he joined the English Department in 2012 as a graduate student largely on the strength of his paper, *The Song of the Phallus: Gender Identity Issues in Fifties Television Situation Comedy.*

He was well known for packing auditoriums during his first two decades at the school with notoriously easy courses that included viewings of such vintage television programs as *Leave It to Beaver* and *Three's Company*, followed by what the syllabus described as "an analysis from a Marxist, feminist, and genderqueered perspective."

In 2017, a conservative student's covert cell phone video of him went viral, getting over three million views. It showed him spending 15 tearful minutes apologizing to one of his sociology classes for "being an unconscious participant in the calculated system of male patriarchal, heteronormative oppression" and, specifically, "for this accursed penis I must bear." After being auto tuned and remixed by an enterprising DJ in Dubrovnik, a version of the rant, entitled "Accursed Penis," backed by heavy bass and drums, became a minor dance club hit, reaching number four on the Serbo-Croatian music charts.

Today he is particularly unhappy. It is his last day at Duke. He was terminated when only three students signed up for his seminar, "Hip Hop Music and American Racism: Voices of Funky Resistance" — and two dropped it before the first class.

Tenure used to protect scholars like me who perhaps did work that challenged the dominant paradigm. The conservatives invaded this safe space and eliminated it.

They ruined the university—they ruined the whole *idea* of a university as a place where intellectuals like myself were able to think about and write on important academic subjects without having to be "productive" [*Professor Windbridge pauses to emphasize the word with air quotes*] or to respond to the so-called "needs" of the students.

The conservatives started by cutting funding to academia. They said we weren't preparing students for the real world. My work is not about getting some privileged white male a job. It's about building consciousness to the racism, sexism, and homophobia that permeates every facet of society. When student loans were cut by these fascists, suddenly students had to pay more of their own expenses and they started forgoing classes like mine that focused on social justice for ones that could get them employed. Ridiculous!

Pretty soon I was being asked to do online courses, but that cut into my academic studies. I'd been working on my magnum opus, *The Male Vagina: Poetry and Dance as a Counterpoint to Phallocentrism*, for six years and I needed to devote my time to finishing it, not to teaching students. We had adjuncts for doing that.

Well, when the new dean—a damn conservative!—told us he was ending tenure and we'd have to demonstrate a positive costs/benefits ratio every year to stay on, well, we told him we would all quit.

And that bastard looked at us and said, "Great. Let me help you pack, because for every one of you there are ten other hacks with doctorates in bullshit studies who'd love to have your jobs at half the pay." He called us "hacks"! Can you imagine?

Well, we stayed, but of course we made that sacrifice only for the students' sake.

12

THE CONSERVATIVE ALTERNATIVE

"We Had Ideas, and the Liberals *Hated* That"

With the election of a conservative president and a conservative Congress in 2024, conservatives had achieved the goal of every guerrilla movement and assumed real power. Now they would act—sometimes ruthlessly—to not only transition the government back to one of small ends and limited means but to ensure that the left could not seize control again.

The insurgency succeeded because it didn't limit itself to one narrow sliver of society. Certainly, actions like targeting academia and other liberal institutions were key over the long term, but those were tactics. The strategy, to the extent there was a strategy, was to change the culture, because if you changed the culture you prevented rollback in the institutions.

It was not merely about replacing constitutional conservatives in the top posts in the institutions. It was about creating a culture that defaulted to constitutional conservative values. But doing that meant operating under the radar until they were ready to strike. And then it meant retaking the institutions the Gramscians had overtaken a generation before.

■ ■ ■

Tony "Gator" McCoy (Chief Advisor to President Carrie Marlowe)

In the White House with President Marlowe, we intended from day one to make conservative change permanent. Marlowe had us aggressively move to consolidate conservative power by exploiting her legislative majorities both in Congress and the states. We had a lot of work to do undoing the damage—we had to literally revoke thousands of executive orders, fire thousands of bureaucrats, and remake the Supreme Court even as we faced down Iran.

But in the first term we pushed through constitutional amendments to expand gun rights, to eliminate racial distinctions, and to enshrine in law the principle that Americans are individually responsible for their own support—not the government. The Thirtieth, Thirty-First, and Thirty-Second Amendments are her real legacy.

We had come through two decades of hardball against us and we didn't hesitate to play it ourselves. We could have pretended the prior 16 years didn't happen—that the left had not eliminated the filibuster, tried to rule by decree, packed the courts, and ignored the Bill of Rights. Some folks wanted us to do that, to return to normal.

But "normal" was not just clearing the slate so as soon as some new liberal Caesar comes along they can do it all over again. No, they changed the rules, and they were going to pay for it. And they did.

I'd be happy to live in a world of handshakes and smiles and bipartisanship, but the liberals killed that unicorn. We drove its horn into their hearts.

David Chang (Conservative Media Host)

The Thirty-Second Amendment was very simple in its text but earth-shaking in its implications for the country and society. It reads:

> Each American shall be presumed to be responsible for the financial support of himself or herself, and for his or her dependents, and Congress shall make no law providing for such support for more than a minimal period of no more than three months during their lives, and in modest amounts necessary to preserve life, unless such person has paid into, and is eligible to participate in, a system of social insurance for such support, is truly and demonstrably physically or mentally unable to support himself or herself, or is injured in the service of this Nation.

Upon its ratification (with the final necessary state being Tennessee) on April 2, 2028, the Thirty-Second Amendment completely upended the progressives' vision of the role of government. The effect of the Thirty-Second Amendment was dramatic. During the second term of the Obama administration, one American in every 6.5 was receiving food stamps. Now, the food stamps program is completely dismantled, as are all cash payments to able-bodied adults. Only Social Security was protected—that would be reformed separately later.

223

Repealing Obamacare was a big step, but the Thirty-Second Amendment was a true watershed. The Thirty-Second Amendment represented what I like to call a "core argument" because it was something all conservatives could rally around. You could be gay or be uncomfortable with gays, or be a believer or be an atheist, you could like abortion or hate it, but you could all get behind the Thirty-Second.

Now, we had a clear statement that the role of government was not to support its citizens except in the narrowest of circumstances—that this was an individual responsibility. We expect you to work. If you make stupid choices, we expect you to work harder

Progressives wanted to try to give you everything, but they could never give you dignity. That's what we give you, and we do it by letting you stand on your own two feet. And, of course, we cut out of the budget most everything else that couldn't be justified under one of the federal government's enumerated powers in the Constitution.

We didn't take power for power's sake. We had ideas, and the liberals *hated* that.

The federal government today is a fraction of its old size, much cheaper, and since it does so much less there is significantly less opportunity for graft and rent-seeking. Most Americans think this is great. Liberals, of course, think we're worse than the Nazis.

Jerome Timms (Republican Congressman)

One of the first things President Marlowe did was sign the minimum mandatory sentences repeal bill, but then she went further and ordered a mass review of all federal drug sentences. She pardoned thousands, including my mom. My mom finally came home after seven years in jail. Our family was back together, but for many other families it was too late. They were broken forever.

Until President Marlowe came along, presidents had rarely used their pardon power, and only after long, bureaucratic investigations. Why take a political risk if you pardon someone who goes and commits another crime? But President Marlowe didn't care about the risk to her at the polls. She cared about doing what was right. She didn't just release people willy-nilly—these were nonviolent offenders—but she took a risk no liberal ever would to try and put families and communities back together.

Then President Marlowe came to the community, but what I noticed was that she hardly said a thing. She sat in a school auditorium filled with local people and *listened*. It was supposed to go an hour. She stayed for three, just listening.

Hillary never listened *to* us. She, and all the liberals, talked *at* us, like she was our savior there to throw us some crumbs. President Marlowe was humble. Then President Marlowe signed off on school choice and I ended up at a magnet school. I worked my way into Harvard and Harvard Law with a scholarship for poor kids with good grades.

I remember how one day, my mom took the Obama photo off our wall and put up one of President Marlowe.

Becky O'Hara (The Last Secretary of Education)

Becky O'Hara is cleaning out her office, but unlike her rival during her first school board election race nearly three decades ago, it is because O'Hara was victorious. She's leaving as the Department of Education itself is closed down, its duties returning to the states where they always belonged.

She points to a framed photo still hanging on the wall of her and the group of parents who took over that suburban Maryland school district about 28 years ago and launched her career as a conservative education reformer.

We were just regular folks, normal Americans, taking an interest in their government. I was a housewife, but the people who ran things thought I was nothing. They thought I didn't matter. They thought they could just ignore us. They thought we were nothing.

They thought wrong. In America, you're only nothing if you let yourself be nothing.

Tamara Hayes Smith (Professor/Activist)

Decades ago there had been a kind of consensus, bipartisan status quo inside the Beltway. There were minor changes at the margins, but both sides generally resisted radical change that would kneecap the other side. Under Obama and Clinton, that changed.

Progressives did not seek to simply beat conservatives in a few elections but to utterly destroy them by using all of their political and cultural power. The constitutional conservatives came into power in the 2020s not knowing any other way to be besides ruthless, and they acted to alter the playing field permanently with aggressive lawmaking, appointing extremely conservative judges, punishing liberal institutions, and even amending the Constitution in dramatic ways.

Conservative were interested in destroying progressivism, and they largely succeeded. Liberals learned that if you try to kill the king, you better succeed.

Barry Sawyer (Radio Host/Political Prisoner)

One of the first things President Marlowe did after being sworn in was pardon Sawyer and everyone else convicted under the censorship laws. Then the president appointed him to the Fairness Commission—with orders to shut it down.

You should have seen their faces. I was public enemy number one to these bureaucrats one day and the next day I am their boss. There were over 1,000 federal employees at the Fairness Commission, and they would have added several thousand more in the next year if the Democrats had won the election.

I know. I read their planning memos. It was going to be an American Stasi.

They even had a SWAT team—I think pretty much every agency used to—and they carried the same weapons they tried to ban citizens from owning.

I gathered all of the employees together in the cafeteria that first morning after I was confirmed. They were really angry, which I found kind of funny since I was the one who had been in jail for 18 months because of them for saying things the government didn't approve of.

Anyway, I walked to the front, and they are all looking at me, and I introduced myself. Silence. Then I said, "You're fired. Pack your personal effects and be out of the building by noon." Then I walked out.

Of course, I had security there to make sure they didn't make off with anything incriminating—they tried, though. We found

227

people with papers and files stuck in their clothes. And I had my tech guys turn off the computer system that morning—totally off—so no one could erase anything.

It was good that we took those precautions. The materials we found outlining how the Clinton administration had waged a war on people who exercised their First Amendment rights were some of the most important evidence we offered at the Political Repression Truth and Reconciliation Commission hearings.

Rob Patel (President-Elect)

In changing American culture, conservatives found themselves changing as well. During our discussion, the president-elect was remarkably open about the fact that he has changed many of his views over time.

I didn't like pot or gay marriage, but I chose not to make those my defining issues and to find common ground with people who felt differently. These let me build larger, stronger coalitions as a congressman and a senator. But it also caused some dissension within our coalition.

You can disagree with people on a few issues and still work with them. I was about 90 percent there with the people who we used to call the "social conservatives" during the Hillary years. I'd say I'm about 95 percent with them now, but that's partly because they've moved my way. For example, the gay marriage fight was huge 30 years ago and it's completely dead now—it's irrelevant.

But it wasn't the social issues that made up the big cultural changes we saw. It was, mostly, the fact that we moved from a society where the expectation was that you were entitled to something to a society where you were expected to earn it for yourself. That was the real central change—a move back toward individual autonomy balanced by individual responsibility. All the other stuff was really just superficial.

Sister Margaret Feeney (Nun/Religious Rights Activist)

The Catholic Church—and other nonliberal sects—rose up to become major centers of resistance to progressive tyranny. Initially, many Catholics were reluctant to sign on to constitutional conservatism, but then they saw that the alternative was for each group resisting the left to be defeated individually if they did not stand together.

I'd say I was about 65 percent in line with the constitutional conservatives, but the other side was 110 percent against me. I could reason with one and be able to worship God as I saw fit, or with the other I could submit in exchange for whatever small bit of religious freedom they deigned to grant me. It was an easy decision.

I still have some heartburn with how focused the constitutional conservatives are on individual action. I think that as a society, we do need to help the needy—I have been doing that for many years. But I began to see the price liberals exacted for doing so.

With them, government was not merely helping people. It was controlling them. Any aid we received at the food kitchen came with strings attached, and those strings always meant liberal government getting into our affairs.

I am much more open to the idea of individual responsibility today. You cannot be free if you are not standing on your own feet—even when someone comes to my food kitchen, they have to hear me preach, then help clean up. That's the price, and I am not somehow wrong to charge it. Nothing is free.

But when government does it, it's not something that brings people closer to God. It's something that makes them bound to the government. It becomes about the power of the state, and we have seen that the state always grows to abuse its power. That's why I've come to believe that government should be as small as possible.

13

PROGRESSIVE REACTIONARIES

"They Didn't Let a Little Thing Like the Constitution Stop Them from Trying to Shut Us Up"

They didn't just surrender. The liberals fought back, using some of the classic techniques of counterinsurgents while making many of the classic mistakes of counterinsurgents that allowed their enemies to flourish.

Liberalism had grown complacent, convinced that the levers of power it controlled were the only levers of power in society. The liberals were wrong. The insurgents resisted.

There was occasional violence. Conservatives baited and teased the left, inviting overreaction that would create a moral crisis for both regular citizens and even some of the left's less ideological members. Censorship, NSA surveillance, IRS harassment, and other un-American acts alienated many of the left's own allies while encouraging the conservatives. The insurgency focused on the people.

Liberalism forgot about the people, focusing only on the elites and their cronies, leaving a vacuum the conservatives eagerly filled.

The two Obama terms and the two Clinton terms were unmitigated disasters for America that the Democratic Party is still trying to live down. In many ways, the 16 years of liberal government tore the scales from the eyes of many Americans who had once believed themselves liberal. Liberal failure—both domestically and internationally—provided an invaluable opportunity for the insurgency.

The American people found their economy stagnant, their nation's reputation and power abroad diminished, and their freedoms at home increasingly under attack. The bailout and the stimulus of the first Obama term started the fire; the lies about Obamacare and its slow disintegration fanned the flames. The conservatives always had an alternative to offer; it was liberal failure that gave the insurgents a chance to show that conservatism was the only alternative.

■ ■ ■

Lieutenant Jim Gallegos (Iranian War Vet)

The former Marine earned his Purple Heart when Iranian bullets tore into him during the ill-fated Operation Urgent Unicorn invasion of the Iranian coast. Gallegos's unit's mission was to seize an oil refinery, but the plan was confused and interference from Clinton administration officials back in Washington prevented the already hollowed-out military forces from holding their objectives.

When Hillary Clinton decided she needed a boost, she suddenly got serious about Iran. By then the military was gutted—no money to train or maintain or sustain, we used to say—and all to pay for spending on her deadbeat voter base. Protecting the country is in the Constitution; sending welfare checks to losers in Fort Living Room isn't. But we were warriors, and we saluted and drove on.

When it went down and we went into Iran to grab some petroleum sites as a "measured response" to nuking our ally, well, we knew it would be a freaking disaster. All these geniuses who never spent a day in uniform were trying to stage-manage the whole thing from DC. We asked for armor. Denied. We asked for air support. Denied.

"Too provocative," the Clinton people said. We were landing on the Iranians' beaches! It doesn't get any more provocative!

Then, when things started going south, they panicked back in the White House.

We didn't. We fought until we ran out of ammo, which was soon because we couldn't get resupplied. Those of us who weren't dead got taken prisoner, paraded on TV—you saw it. The world laughed at us. Clinton made Jimmy Carter look like George Patton—her groveling apology from the Oval Office begging the mullahs to let us go was the last thing we wanted to hear, as much as we wanted to get home.

Then the Iranians told her that wasn't enough, and she looked like an even bigger clown. When President Marlowe got inaugurated and gave her "you have 24 hours" speech—holy shit, the Iranians did a 180. They knew she was deadly serious. We got nice new clothes, some real food, and we were out of that shithole of a country in under 24 hours.

Tony "Gator" McCoy (Chief Advisor to President Carrie Marlowe)

The first thing we did was deal with Iranian prisoner crisis that had paralyzed the Clinton administration. It was just like

233

what Reagan did in 1981. We did it in a distinctly conservative fashion.

The president walked to the podium and announced, "This a message to Iran's leaders. You have 24 hours to have all American prisoners out of Iranian airspace or the United States will commence unrestricted warfare upon your nation with the intention of destroying your military and secret police, annihilating your infrastructure, and killing you specifically. This is not threat—it is a promise. I will not be taking any questions. Iran now has 23 hours, 59 minutes and 30 seconds." Then she walked off.

The press was stunned. The people, though, went nuts supporting her. Here's the thing—she would have done it. The military, as screwed over as it was from 16 years of liberal administrations, was set to act.

I can't say much about the war plan because it's still classified, but have you ever seen a parking lot? Now think of one that's made of glass and glows in the dark.

Rudy Zamora (Major, Texas Rangers)

He looks like the picture of a rough-and-tumble Western lawman even when he is dressed for golf. We are at a course outside Fort Stockton, a west Texas town that used to be known as a pit stop on Interstate 10 and today is a growing city feeding off the oil boom that never seems to end thanks to environmental deregulation.

Rudy Zamora is soft-spoken, but don't let that fool you. He was the lead Texas Ranger at the "Battle of Austin" in 2021. Zamora retired in 2028, moved to Fort Stockton, and was soon elected mayor. If you look carefully, you can see the outline of his pistol in his waistband under his shirt.

I am a Texan. Yeah, I'm also an American—I fought in Iraq—but this is a republic. It's built on principles. The Constitution sets those out, and I figure the Bill of Rights ought to mean what it says. So when the Clinton administration went after our governor for refusing to enforce the new federal gun laws, I had no problem when I got ordered to stop it.

Hillary slipped through in 2020—she didn't win Texas, that's for sure—but I think she figured her crew was going to lose the next time. She and her pals were bound and determined to beat us into line before she had to go. She did a lot of bad things. The worst was when her handpicked Supreme Court came out and said that the Second Amendment that says we Americans can keep and bear arms really doesn't say that. They found a lot of things the Constitution didn't say in there, but they couldn't see the things it did say.

Well, that stirred us up pretty good, but Texas law still protected our rights. Hillary hated that—she hated the entire South, especially Texas. So she jammed through a bill requiring citizens to turn in their "assault weapons"—which weren't assault weapons—and register all the rest.

And she expected us to play along. She expected us to just roll over. After all, it seemed like people had been rolling over to DC liberals for decades.

She didn't know Texans. It just wasn't going to happen.

Our governor announced that we wouldn't cooperate. Not only won't we do it, he says, but we won't let the feds enforce the law in Texas.

Well, now everyone is looking at us because we've drawn a line. The liberal media is getting spun up about "the new insurrectionists" and all, but the people of Texas were behind the governor—even a lot of Texas Democrats.

Sometimes you gotta call out a bully. Hillary was a bully, and we called her out. So she had a problem. And I don't think she really thought through what she did next.

She had her attorney general go into a federal court back in DC and get one of the judges Obama packed it with to issue an order holding our governor in contempt. Then the attorney general announced that the governor was going to be arrested by federal law enforcement.

By this time, we're watching all the federal agencies in the state. Many of the feds were sympathetic, so we knew right away that an order had come from Washington into the US marshal's office in Dallas. It ordered the lead deputy US marshal to go arrest the governor and put him in the federal lockup in Dallas. I know how the deputy responded to Washington: "Do you want a massacre? The hell I will." And he and his people sat tight in their offices.

I know the FBI refused to arrest him as well. I got a call from a friend at the Houston field office, and I told him this was a bad idea. He passed it back to headquarters. The FBI director personally told the attorney general it was not within their jurisdiction, but the truth was that the FBI just wasn't going to kick that hornet's nest.

So, the attorney general was furious because none of her people in Texas would go and arrest the governor. She wouldn't listen to them when they told her this was some serious shit, that the Texans weren't just going to sit back and take it. That's why you don't put a law professor who has never lived outside of Boston in a position like AG—you need to have some understanding of the country you live in if you want to be its chief federal law-enforcement officer.

Obama and Clinton and their crew had been so used to just doing what they wanted they forgot that at the heart of things, America works only because everyone agrees the system is legitimate and cooperates. They tossed away legitimacy but expected us to act like they hadn't. That was a recipe for disaster.

We got word that the Marshals Service had chartered a 737 jet and that a big team was flying into Austin at 11:22 p.m. on May 1, 2021. I talked to the governor beforehand and told him my plan. He said he didn't want any of us to risk ourselves because of him.

"It isn't about you, sir" I said. It was about principles. I told him I'd try to avoid trouble, but I was a Ranger and I wasn't going to run from it.

We went up into the control tower and tried to warn them off. They told us they were landing anyway. The AG had made sure they picked guys who would do whatever they were ordered to do—a dozen deputies back in DC actually got fired for refusing to go.

We knew they were heavily armed; they thought they were going to intimidate us. They didn't understand Texans, I guess. By dawn, they did.

We made sure the controllers knew where to direct the jet on the airfield once it landed. I deployed my sniper teams to cover the tarmac and brought up a few dozen vehicles to pen in the plane. We figured there were about 20 feds on the plane—turned out to be 33—so I brought over 100 personnel. Yeah, I know, "One riot, one Ranger," but I figured they were less likely to try to play horsey if we outnumbered them.

Only a few of us were Rangers. Most of us were actually Department of Public Safety officers or other local law enforcement. I was a major in the Rangers, and I had operational control of the operation.

I wouldn't let our guys gear up like they were getting ready for World War III, but they did have their gear out of sight nearby just in case. I wanted to work this out peacefully, and you do that by deescalating the situation whenever you can.

Then it starts to go down. The plane lands and the controllers guide it right to where we wanted it. A few more units drive out and surround it. The plane is now totally closed in.

We send one of those ladder trucks up to the door and I go to the foot to wait. My men are behind the vehicles surrounding the aircraft, weapons out of sight. I'm maybe 25 meters out front. I have an earpiece in and I have comms with everyone, including my snipers. I had my issue .357 SIG Sauer, and I had a couple extra 12-round mags just in case. I was hoping not to have to use them.

At that point, before the door opened, I'm still pretty sure I'll be able to talk those boys into turning around and flying back home. But they had other ideas.

The first guy out is Deputy Raymond Hough, who I knew in the past from some joint fugitive investigations. I didn't think much of him, to be honest. He comes down the ramp with a bunch of his boys and they're decked out for war. Armor, helmets, M4s. My guys see it too, and I can hear the chatter in my earpiece. I whisper, "Relax. Just keep your heads and this will all work out."

The feds were trying to show me that they came to play, so I just kept calm.

Hough is all in black—they were all in black. Right off, he tells me, "You and your men are obstructing a federal law-enforcement operation! If you don't stand down, you'll be arrested!"

I say, "Now Ray, you seem to be a little outnumbered here. Why don't we talk this over?"

"Nothing to talk about," he says. "We're here to do a job, and we're doing it."

Now, more of his guys are coming off the plane, stepping past me and Hough, and fanning out. My guys are keeping calm, but these feds are all carrying heavy weapons and they are getting jumpy.

I don't like how it's going, so I say, "Ray, maybe you can ask your boys to get back on the plane and we can talk about this. There are a lot of guys with weapons out here, and you know how one stupid move can send things out of control real quick."

But Hough wasn't listening. They'd been trained to use overwhelming force to dominate the situation, and they were reverting to their training. They were trying to dominate a situation they didn't have control over. My guys were just standing off, behind their vehicles, heavy weapons out of sight. But the feds were spreading out to confront them.

"At least tell your guys to sling their rifles, Ray," I said.

But he wasn't having any of it. He goes, "Get your fucking state troopers out of our way, Zamora. Do it now! Where are our buses?" We had intercepted the buses they chartered and sent them away.

So I say, "You're not leaving this airfield, Deputy. Now, how about we do this the smart way?"

Then he says, "How about I cuff your ass?"

I kept trying to turn the heat down. "I figure that'll be a bad idea, Ray. Let's not get stupid," I say.

239

But even as I was talking, about 75 meters away a deputy marshal named Wayne Grohl was in a staring contest with a Texas state trooper named David Rodriguez. Grohl lived, though with a few holes in him, and testified that Deputy Rodriguez was making a move on him. The camera footage shows that never happened. The deputy never even put his hand on his service weapon. Grohl shot him in the face, and all hell broke loose.

The feds heard Grohl's shot and just opened up on us. They had their rifles up already, so for a couple seconds they had the advantage. Our guys on the tarmac dropped behind their vehicles and went for their own heavy weapons, but a couple got hit on the way down.

I saw what happened and yelled for Hough to call "cease fire," but he was either stupid or pumped with adrenaline or both, because he turns and brings his M4 up at me.

One of my snipers took off most of his head.

Hough staggers and falls. Now bullets are flying everywhere and I've got two problems. First, I'm 25 meters in front of my men and their barricade of vehicles out in the middle of a bunch of stupid, scared feds. Second, and worse, with Hough dead, there's no one in charge of the feds to get them to stop shooting.

I don't recall drawing my SIG—years of training made it instinctive, I guess—but it's in my hand when a young fed comes out behind the stairway and sees me. I yell "Get down," but he starts taking a bead on me.

I took aim center mass and fired—right into the Kevlar plate I knew he was wearing. I knew it wouldn't penetrate, but the .357 slug did knock him on his ass. Broke a couple ribs, but kept him out of the fight. First guy whose life I ever saved by shooting him in the chest.

Bullets are whizzing around. I can hear brass falling from the door of the jet and hitting the tarmac around me from the guys shooting up there. Now our guys are firing back and tearing the jet up—bullets are punching into the sheet metal and cracking the windows. I'm crouching by the stairway just trying not to get shot as I try to retake control.

"Cease fire! Cease fire!" I'm yelling into my comms, but when somebody's shooting at you, you know, you shoot him. There were about 12 feds on the tarmac when Grohl fired and pretty soon every one of them was down, either dead or wounded.

I saw a marshal in the door of the aircraft firing full auto and then take one in the neck and fall backwards. Then the firing petered out.

After a couple minutes, we started talking to the guys on the plane. It wasn't flying anywhere, that was for sure. It looked like Swiss cheese, so we needed to figure out what to do with the survivors. Eventually, they gave up their weapons and we kept them in a hotel until we could bus them out. They weren't prisoners—except for Grohl.

I'm not proud of what happened there. It makes me sick. But I did my duty, and I gotta say I'm happy I didn't have to kill anyone myself. I know it broke up the Texans who did. It's bad enough killing a bad man. Another cop, even one who is enforcing unconstitutional laws? It makes you want to throw up. We killed nine United States marshals and wounded eight more. They killed one Texas Ranger, a guy who had been in my wedding, and one state trooper, Deputy Rodriguez, plus wounded six more. It was a tragedy, and it was all the Clinton administration's doing.

Now, the administration was stunned. This was something entirely new—active resistance. They immediately claimed we

241

"ambushed" the marshals and the mainstream media parroted that line. We weren't dumb, though. We had cameras all over the place, and our governor let the administration tie itself into a false story, then called a press conference. Even the mainstream media had to show up for that—this was huge news, flood-the-zone coverage.

He had me walk through the events using our footage, which the public had not seen until then, and it was very clear that the feds escalated the situation and started shooting, and there was no doubt at all that the administration was lying.

Of course Hillary threw the attorney general under the bus. The AG resigned, and her replacement negotiated with us, dropping the contempt order. The administration also agreed not to try and enforce the new gun laws in any state that refused to allow it, and 32 states refused. We gave them back Deputy Marshal Grohl instead of trying him for murder ourselves. They let him plead guilty to a federal manslaughter charge.

Right after the shootout, we were not sure what to expect next. There was a lot of talk about "civil war," but that was foolishness. No one wanted any more real fighting. Our country had deep problems, but we needed to solve them using the means in the Constitution. It was the Clinton administration ignoring the Constitution that had got us where we were in the first place.

Plus, the administration suddenly realized that it might not have the means to fight, if it came to that. Some of its own law-enforcement personnel had refused to participate in the Texas operation, and who knows what a conservative, largely Southern military would do if she gave it an unlawful order.

One more thing. Antigun legislation in liberal states had driven gun and gun accessory makers to the free states, away from the Northeast and West Coast. That's the opposite of the Civil War, where the Yankees had all the gun factories. The conservative states supplied most of the warriors and most of the weapons. In the end, what were the liberals going to do, make us submit with harsh language?

Darren Dolby (Lawyer/Activist)

This flamboyant attorney talks about the Clinton administration's gun laws and the grassroots reaction to them, with widespread resistance by police who refused to cooperate (sometimes because of state laws instructing them not to) and by jury nullification.

We started up a campaign to inform potential jurors in the trials of those charged with possessing weapons to vote to acquit regardless of the evidence—to nullify the law through a refusal by jurors to enforce it. This brought on a backlash by the Clinton administration as it tried to ban our attempts to discuss nullification.

We were also all over that, highlighting the anti–free speech agenda of the progressives. They didn't let a little thing like the Constitution stop them from trying to shut us up. They even got the Supreme Court to rule they could do it, which we got overturned later. But this whole thing eroded support among the left's own allies, who were queasy at the thought of jailing people for speaking out and eliminating the right to trial by jury.

There were two kinds of liberals: the principled liberals and the power liberals. The principled liberals had a crisis—they saw that the Obama and Clinton administrations weren't honoring the principles these liberals believed in. They had to choose,

243

them or us. Many chose us—the constitutional conservative movement had a lot of ex-liberals.

And the power liberals? Principles were a means to an end. When a principle stopped being useful, they had no compunction about dropping it. With them, no matter what the administrations did—intimidate, harass, and even arrest critics—it didn't matter. They didn't believe in anything but their own power. They could never be reasoned with. They had to be defeated.

Brad Fields (Insurance Salesman)

It was a scary time. The liberals were literally putting folks in jail for speaking out against them, though neither they nor their media lackeys would describe it that way. They called it "campaign finance reform," basically saying that free speech of any kind could be regulated. Of course, what's regulated can be banned. And that's what they tried to do to our conservative Internet and radio content.

They were also trying to take people's guns, breaking into houses without warrants. There were some incidents besides Texas . . . it was bad. There was talk of violence. But the violence came from the left. Union and leftist thugs would physically attack people who criticized the administration— sometimes the thugs would burn their houses—and the feds wouldn't do anything even when everyone saw on video the people doing it.

One liberal punk, some 29-year-old in Washington, wrote a column in the *Post* calling on Hillary Clinton to execute people for interfering with her agenda. He said flat out that the conservatives had no right to free speech or assembly or the press and that she should do whatever she had to do to stop us, including shoot us. But first, she should disarm us. We were committing "treason" by opposing her, he said. This ran in a major newspaper, and many, many liberals applauded it.

The Iran fiasco just made it worse. The Clinton administration was getting paranoid. Regular people like me were worried that we could find police at our door. I think if they had had more faith that law enforcement and the military would have carried it out, there would have been even worse repression.

It was a very ugly time. But there was a lot of camaraderie among conservatives. We took the Constitution seriously. We paid attention and fought for it when it was in danger.

Ted Jindal (Technology Consultant)

Some of Jidaltech's most successful products have been security software founder Ted Jindal worked to develop as he fought to protect insurgent information systems from constant attacks by opponents. He recalls how liberals did whatever they could to stop his work.

We got hacked a lot, on a systematic basis. This wasn't just random leftists, though that was always a problem. It was a concerted effort paid for by anonymous donors to go in and try to destroy our computer systems and databases. I can't tell you how I know, and I categorically deny that we retaliated with our own hack attacks.

They turned the feds on us, and the Clinton Justice Department was only too happy to prosecute us for hacking . . . alleged hacking. Thankfully, the juries kept hanging in my case until the prosecutors just gave up. Thank goodness for the jury

245

nullification campaign. The liberals hated it, but it was a great weapon to at least partially neutralize the campaign of political prosecutions we saw during those years.

They were playing for keeps, but so were we.

Barry Sawyer (Radio Host/Political Prisoner)

Sawyer was a conservative shock jock who owned a radio network. After the 2019 Media Fair Play Act set up the Fairness Commission to regulate radio content, he not only refused to comply with orders to cut the time devoted to conservative talk but made a huge deal about refusing to do so. He forced the feds to act heavy-handedly—a key insurgent tactic.

When the federal marshals arrived to arrest me, I made sure there were plenty of cameras around to record the event. The photos of me in chains being hauled away for refusing government orders about what I could and could not broadcast flashed across the Internet even as the mainstream media attempted to ignore it.

I was sentenced to prison, and the leftist Supreme Court upheld my conviction, but I made a decision to become a martyr for free speech—and my incarceration created enormous doubts even within the liberal coalition. Some of them actually believed in things like free speech. Others, not so much.

Gail Partridge (Leftist Show Host)

Outraged at the success of the conservative insurgents in fighting back, she vents about people like Barry Sawyer.

I am all for free speech, but what they were doing wasn't free speech. It was sedition!

They lied about the government to interfere with its programs, and I don't see why that was tolerated so much. Hillary should have done more to stand up to them. It's not free speech when you abuse that right to damage efforts toward social justice and progress. The legitimate Supreme Court, before the coup, agreed.

I don't feel sorry at all for these criminals. That's what they were, criminals. The law was very clear and they broke it. Hillary was absolutely right not to let a bunch of racist, rich, wreckers hide behind some 250-year-old scrap of paper.

14

HOW HOLLYWOOD WENT CONSERVATIVE

"The Gatekeepers Found Themselves Guarding the Gates While the Walls Were Tumbling Down Around Them"

The late Andrew Breitbart identified the entertainment industry as a key center of gravity for the progressive project, so much so that he started a conservative website, *Big Hollywood*, devoted to chronicling its antics. But even as the industry came under pressure to diversify and change, it remained stubbornly resistant—that is, until technology and some old-fashioned political hardball, plus artists who simply refused to be pigeonholed, forced it to evolve.

■ ■ ■

Joe Farris (Filmmaker)

Joe Farris started making films during the Obama administration. Today, he runs a production company turning out popular movies and video programing. He doesn't look like what conservatives are supposed to look like—he still has long hair, and his office echoes with what he describes as "nü nü-metal" music. However, he has little use for liberalism in general, or for liberals themselves.

We started out in a crappy apartment in St. Louis, where I was from. We thought we ought to go to Hollywood, but we didn't have any money. We had just enough cash for some cameras and our computers and Internet access. We would make these little short videos and edit them with software we downloaded for free. We'd finish cutting them and then post it on our YouTube Channel.

Our stuff wasn't political at first, or what we thought of as political. We were trying to be funny, because funny means hits. So did cats. We kept trying to think of a really funny political cat video because we knew that would go viral. Never did, though.

I was never political before, but I was very much about freedom—especially on the web. I was really pissed off to read about how the NSA under Obama was gathering all sorts of Internet tracking info. I thought that they, being liberals, should be against that sort of thing. But they weren't.

We were doing pretty well, getting a reputation. We'd put something up and get 50,000 hits in a day. The next time, we would shoot for 100,000. It was still a new thing back then for a bunch of nobodies with a little bit of equipment to be able to get an audience.

Now, we would play off of other material in our political stuff—you can't satirize something without referencing it, right? But we'd get all this copyright grief. Studios and companies would demand YouTube and other sites pull our stuff for infringement, and they would. But it wasn't infringement—it was fair use, like our lawyers told us, but there was nothing stopping these big companies from throwing their weight around to screw us over.

Funny, but I first thought it was conservatives doing it. You know, big business equaled conservative? So I was totally sideswiped when I did some research and found out that the liberals were backing these big companies over little guys like us. The only people sticking up for us on Internet freedom were the constitutional conservatives. It kind of freaked me out. I thought I hated the Tea Party and it turns out we agreed on a lot of stuff that was important to me.

So, we started tweaking the left for hypocrisy. Some of our viewers didn't like it because we were not, you know, on the team. Well, I don't play on teams—I do what I want. But, because our videos weren't afraid of taking on liberals, we got a reputation as conservative.

I thought that was going to limit us as far as getting an audience, but things were changing. The old ways of doing business were dying. I was reaching millions of people with my work and it had never been on TV or in a movie. The dinosaurs in Hollywood couldn't ignore us anymore—they were getting desperate because people were going around them to get the media product they refused to provide.

We got an e-mail from an agent in Hollywood. He actually said that he wanted "to do lunch"—he used those exact words! I'm not sure what was funnier—him using that phrase or him just assuming we had to be in his town to do what we did. Like I said, the established Hollywood types just did not understand the changes overcoming their industry.

I called him on the phone and broke the bad news to him, first that I was half a continent away and second that we were

251

conservative. He was more worried about where we were. He said that with the kind of traffic our videos were getting, he'd meet with us if we were the Khmer Rouge.

Technology totally opened the doors to the entertainment industry, which I think was and is probably the most important element of American culture. It's a battlefield we had no choice but to go fight on as conservatives. For too long we left most of it—with exceptions like country music—to the cultural left. And we paid for it.

The old entertainment industry was built on several structural factors. First, they produced product—movies, TV, records, books—that required a huge capital outlay for equipment and for professionals to use it. Studios, cameras, recording equipment, printing presses, and highly paid people to use them cost a fortune.

That was a huge barrier to entry in the past. Back then, those independents who did do their own work often ended up making things like *Plan 9 from Outer Space* and all those terrible DIY punk records people used to sell out of their Gremlin hatchbacks for a buck. My dad told me about those. My generation had a different experience.

Besides money, the majors also controlled the distribution of entertainment. They were gatekeepers. If you wanted to be on TV, in a theater, in a record store, or in a bookstore, you had to go through them. And if they disapproved, you didn't get through at all.

Well, that was all dying right as the conservative movement really got underway. While primo equipment is still pricey, it is possible for nearly any group of entrepreneurs to gather up the money to make their product. We did. And this was a product of pretty high-level technical quality. A lot of what we did was comparable to the stuff produced by the majors. Professionals still had their place, but modern technology made it exponentially simpler to do what it used to take a highly paid pro to do.

The gatekeepers found themselves guarding the gates while the walls were tumbling down around them.

So, we stopped waiting at the gates. We were just going to go around the gates because the walls were collapsing. Sure, only a major studio could open a film at 3,000 theaters, but anybody could get on video on demand. And everyone did—have you seen how many movies you've never heard of are out there? Content is king.

Back when Obama was president, it became possible to watch whatever you wanted whenever you wanted with just a couple clicks of your remote control or on your computer or device. It's normal today, but back then it was incredible.

And we got into the industry with outspoken conservative material. So did a lot of other conservatives. Of course, most of it was crap, but most of everything is crap.

There was a huge opportunity for conservative folks to enter the entertainment industry without waiting on an invitation. By simply making product, they gained visibility. The ones that made good stuff, the ones that found an audience, eventually found the industry eager to take advantage of them. Sure, most of the folks in the entertainment industry were liberal, and probably most still are, but all of them really like money. And if they think a conservative will make them money, he's got a shot.

There was one important principle we needed to learn. There was no room and no market for "conservative entertainment." None. Zip.

There was always room for *quality* entertainment, entertainment that finds an audience because it's good. That it is conservative too is a fringe benefit. Anyone who is trying to make entertainment that tries to be conservative before it's entertaining is going to find that his product sucks before it does anything else.

I remember people would come into Hollywood with a lot of money and announce they wanted to make conservative films. What's a conservative film anyway? I'd say *Saving Private Ryan* or *Dirty Harry* were conservative films from a time when conservatism was frowned upon. But these guys always thought it meant a movie with no action, no sex, no bad words, and no freaking point. Usually, it would have characters talking about Jesus—hey, nothing rocks a theater like 10 minutes of theological exposition.

We'd take their money and help them with the technical aspects of making "conservative movies," but outside that narrow band of conservative audiences, no one else ever saw those productions. It was mostly because they were terrible.

The secret—well, it's not even a secret—is to make good product from a conservative point of view. If it's a comedy, be funny before you are conservative. Drama? Be dramatic first. But it was hard to get that message through to people who thought the answer to liberal agitprop was conservative agitprop. The so-called "conservative" stuff was so dull it didn't even agitate well!

The idea was and is to compete as entertainment. Sure, the industry was largely liberal by default, but we used our quality entertainment as a vehicle to promote our conservative values. Yes, we needed to use popular culture to spread our message and no, it didn't make us as bad as the liberals. Reinforcing positive values and traditions of a society is one of the roles of art, and has been since the ancient Greeks put on plays in their amphitheaters. Popular culture should teach people about their society and, yes, model positive behaviors.

It used to do that before the 1970s, when the liberals really took over. Remember how old movies showed John Wayne as a hero to be copied? In the Obama years, we had movies featuring Seth Rogan—remember him?—as the perpetual man-child covering up his pathetic emasculation with moderately clever snark. Art was still trying to teach people how to be. It was just that liberal art tried to teach them to be losers.

And putting out our point of view was not somehow foisting our views on the audience. Now, I wouldn't mind if we did—our views should be foisted on the audience because our views aren't terrible and socially poisonous like liberal ones.

When we did it to promote constitutional conservatism, it was good. When they did it to promote their liberal fascism, it was bad. There's no moral equivalence because only our side is moral. I saw how liberalism acts in power—when it wasn't corrupt or incompetent, it was crushing our freedoms.

Some subsets of conservatives started getting footholds in the industry. Conservative religious-based entertainment was an outlier, but it spoke to a huge audience that was terribly underserved back then. It just needed to stop being mostly terrible. That came with experience and an understanding that it better be entertaining first or no one will watch.

Conservative-themed reality shows were popular. Many had to do with sports like hunting and shooting, and others had to do with that most conservative of activities, working. Oddly, during the Obama years, there were a lot of shows about guys busting their butts crab fishing, driving trucks, farming, and the like. These were kind of the antithesis of liberal entertainment even if they never mentioned the word "conservative."

But we needed to hit the mainstream. Popular music was full of liberals, but along came some rockers and rappers laying down killer tracks that were thoroughly conservative. I mean, life during the Obama and Clinton administrations was so tough for young people that eventually some of their musical artists were going to have to call out liberalism. When that happened, a bunch of kids started nodding their heads, and it opened a door to them really looking at constitutional conservatives for the first time.

Some popular movies already had subtle conservative elements—if *The Dark Knight Rises* was any more conservative it would have been Ronald Reagan under the cowl. Of course, Christopher Nolan was reluctant to say so publicly. But then some people did—they came out of the right-wing closet. Again, that opened a door to a whole new audience of potential conservatives who had opted out of pop culture.

I kind of did that. I came out, and I got a deal on cable to make what turned out to be the conservative equivalent—in quality of writing and insight—of HBO's feminist show *Girls*. Of course, I made sure we had better nudity. Conservative women are always hotter.

Remember that the value of a pop culture presence is not only (or even mostly) based on the content itself, but what I think of as the normalization factor. The increased conservative presence made conservatives familiar and unthreatening. We stopped being pictured as uterus-obsessed Bible thumpers, and the loss of that caricature was a big blow to our opponents.

Popular culture made constitutional conservatives, if not cool, at least not the face of evil. Conservative normalization was huge.

Drew Johnson (TV Producer)

I met up with veteran situation comedy producer Drew Jordan at the Manhattan Beach Studios soundstage, where he is overseeing production on a new comedy series. The man who helped lead the rise of young, conservative—or at least libertarian—artists is now an elder statesman. He stands back, keeping a close eye on the director and stepping in to add his advice when things get difficult. He is now clearly part of the Hollywood establishment, and it is hard to imagine just how much of a departure his first hit show, *Legal Aid*, represented when it premiered in 2019.

Legal Aid was a show about some attractive young lawyers just out of law school working at a legal aid clinic. Now you'd expect it to be some sort of liberal fantasy about earnest kids helping poor, oppressed victims fight the system. At least that's what we told the network it would be, but instead we took it in a much funnier direction, and one I happened to agree with.

The hero, Baxter, has no patience for losers and in the first scene on the first show this client is whining about how his landlord was evicting him and blah blah blah, and Baxter listens and nods and finally says "Well, here's my legal opinion. Maybe you ought to get your lazy ass a job and pay your rent." And the studio audience loved it.

They'd never heard that before. See, we didn't make Baxter a jerk—we made him a stand-in for every American who had ever worked hard but watched other people game the system and never get held to account. The network panicked, and the critics were furious, but the ratings went through the roof.

Legal Aid helped mainstream conservative characters who

weren't caricatures or villains, and the culture responded. Conservatives stopped being thought of as outside the mainstream because they now were mainstream. A show called *Will & Grace* did that to mainstream gays in the 1990s by showing regular gay folks as normal and nonthreatening. We did that with conservatives. And we stopped making every liberal do-gooder a hero and started showing them as they usually are—bossy, snobby, and under the mistaken impression that they know best how everyone else should live their lives.

Dan Stringer (Billionaire CEO/Activist)

We noticed that there were a ton of really smart, talented people out there trying to use the web to make an impact using the visual arts. And they never had any money, yet they were having an impact.

I set up an organization that would provide microgrants—sometimes a grand or so—or would provide help on web technology to set up sites and stuff. They made films, web series, and all sorts of things. Today, some of them have careers in the industry after getting a start with a microgrant from us.

One bunch of my guys did a web video campaign combined with street art for marijuana decriminalization designed to undercut the liberals with, well, the dope-smoking demographic. This burnout who called himself Puff was the star—he'd say something like, "Getting arrested harshes my buzz, dude!"

It was funny and got a lot of attention, and then when it was revealed it was a bunch of constitutional conservatives behind it, suddenly we started getting taken seriously about our support for a liberty agenda.

This was a huge opportunity for these conservative entrepreneurs—that's what I saw them as: entrepreneurs! Some succeeded, and some failed, but we had a huge return on investment!

Oh, the liberals were furious that I was supporting conservative visual artists, which merely encouraged me! See, politics was only a part. Aiming money at culture was key.

Brad Fields (Insurance Salesman)

I don't want to ban any entertainment—I like a good action scene, and I'm not too old to appreciate a shower scene either. But I don't want to pay to watch something where I'm called "a hater" or "an idiot" or any of those other things they portrayed conservatives as in the past. I just stopped spending my money on liberal crap. When stuff that treated us with respect came out, I started to go out again and I'd see that.

I guess Hollywood finally noticed when we conservatives started to hit it in the wallet.

Tony "Gator" McCoy (Chief Advisor to President Carrie Marlowe)

The president recognized that Hollywood was a threat, so she sent me out to California as the designated "bad cop" to confront the power players. They just didn't get it—they didn't know any of us constitutional conservatives and apparently bought their own propaganda that we were a bunch of inbred, slack-jawed, barely literate racists.

I listened to this one little twerp lecture me for about five minutes on what the Marlowe administration needed to do vis-à-vis their industry, like we owed them anything at all after they savaged her during the campaign. He shut his sushi hole, smirked, and then I asked, "Why again should we do jack shit for you?" They were stunned.

I went on. "You give the other guys money, your shows portray us as assholes and dumbshits, and now you talk to me like I'm one of your latte-fetching flunkies. Listen up. You don't have friend one who can do shit for you inside the Beltway anymore. My guys don't owe you squat—in fact, screwing you is gonna make their voters cheer. So, tell me again why I don't make kicking you in your nutsacks my hobby for the next eight years?"

Now, these guys were all used to hardball, but I was playing dodgeball, and when I play dodgeball I throw *wrenches* instead of balls.

"I just talked to the Speaker. Guess what we decided to bring up next session? Copyright reform. Yeah, you know how you get rights to your little cartoon characters and songs and videos for umpteen years now? We're thinking 10 years is *plenty*. How do you like that? Because we're just getting started."

They were silent—not a freaking peep. They figured out there was a new sheriff in town.

"Okay," I said, "Now that we understand each other, I think we're ready to discuss our future working relationship. And I have a feeling this is going to be the start of a beautiful friendship."

Chis-El (Rapper)

The old-school rapper runs his music and lifestyle empire from a Florida high-rise. The walls in his office are lined with gold records and photos, as well as two portraits: Booker T. Washington and Ronald Reagan.

Seated behind an enormous oak desk, he wears a blazing white suit and dark black glasses. However, his manner is friendly and open—he has just returned from a visit to a youth home his charitable foundation runs in downtown Miami.

The hip-hop impresario was first noted for his infectious 2016 hip-hop smash "Cuz I Split Tha Rock" and a string of other huge hits. Today, he is a full-blown entrepreneur, with clothing lines and other ventures besides a music label that boasts a formidable lineup of talent. He offered a visiting reporter one of his Chis-El Mac cigars, grown and rolled at his plantation in Cuba—Chis-El was among the first businessmen to flood back in after President Marlowe ordered the 2026 surgical invasion that liberated the imprisoned isle from the tyranny of the doddering relics of the Castro regime.

I saw firsthand how welfare poisoned my community. When you make the government the man of the family, you don't leave room for the real man. I take nothing away from the ladies who struggled to raise kids alone, but I was lucky. I had a family with a father. I have a family now, and I am there with them.

I always saw myself as conservative. Most black folk supported the Democrats and things were always getting worse—that made no sense to me. So when I hit it big I was asked on a television interview if I'd be campaigning for Hillary Clinton and I just said, "Hell no. I'm a Republican because I don't believe in welfare. I believe a man supports himself and his own."

A lot of people started talking smack about me but I went right back at them. I don't have to explain myself to fools, but I wanted to make sure my fans understood. And when I asked why it made sense for me to work my ass off so some lazy punk can sit on his ass all day collecting a check, a lot of folks understood.

My biggest selling jam was "Get Your Ass a Job." I told it straight up—if you aren't supporting yourself, you're a punk-ass bitch.

That song blew up. I heard that back in the day, when he was Senator Patel, he had it as his ringtone. People were saying it in the street—it was a catchphrase. I turned on a TV show once and one of the characters said it to some bum. I couldn't take the Katy Perry cover version, though.

I started producing and a lot of folks who thought like I did would expect me to back them, but if they sounded like shit I threw them out. You need to show some talent—it's not enough to agree with me. I wouldn't call a lot of rappers conservative even now, but there are more diverse views. Conservatives upped their game and the good ones made records.

Sammy Honda (Hollywood Producer)

"Hey, babe, we'll do lunch!" producer Sammy Honda says as he pats a noted situation comedy star on the shoulder while moving through the chic West Hollywood restaurant to his reserved table. "That lady is super beautiful, super talented. Love her work. Love it! I mean, she's a damn commie, but you know, it's a free country. You want to be liberal? Hey, you can even be liberal in Hollywood. This is an open-minded community!"

Honda, the producer of such conservative favorite shows as *Deadbeats!* and *Normal Family*, remembers when talking about Hollywood as tolerant of liberals would have gotten him a recommendation that he replace his current psychiatrist. "When I got here in 2010, I said nothing about my politics. Nothing! You couldn't unless you were some sort of leftist, because it seemed everyone was leftist and you'd never work again. But it only seemed that way. This town, then and now, runs on money. If you made money, you generally worked even if your politics would have made Genghis Khan need a hug."

We are seated, and without bothering to consult the menu Honda orders an off-the-menu lettuce salad with chicken, quinoa, cashews, and tomatoes, then double-checks that the tomatoes are organic. "My life coach is very strict about my diet. The tomatoes have to be organic or my chakra gets unbalanced or something. Where were we? Oh, right . . ."

Anyway, there were always a fair number of conservative folks in town, most off screen. Crews were often largely conservative. A lot of business folk and producers too. Some stars were too. Adam Baldwin was very open about his views, and he worked all the time. So was Nick Searcy, who left television to found the Nick Searcy School of Acting and coached I don't know how many Oscar winners—though anyone who comes out of his school is a total prima donna for some reason. Anyway, we always had a few conservatives around.

[The waiter brings Honda a glass of Chablis. He sips and scowls. "I don't know how Chablis ever came back, but everyone's drinking it so I guess it's good and I just don't know it. Where was I? Oh yeah . . ."]

During the conservative comeback, the conservatives started consciously coming to Hollywood. They used to largely write it off, but technology changed and the old distribution channels changed so suddenly the liberals at the studios couldn't gatekeep like they used to.

Wait, I need to take this . . .

263

[*Honda makes no effort to lower his voice as he speaks into his phone about the pioneering conservative comedy series about men under siege by a liberal world that he helped produce. "Cam, my man, here's my idea. Ready? We reboot* Dudes *as a movie . . . Listen, three words. Channing. Tatum. Junior. Hello? You still there? Yeah, well you talk to Jim, then my people will talk to yours. Two words. Ka. Ching! Bye now!"*]

Where was I?

Oh right, you'd get conservatives and they'd make movies for video on demand on the cheap and no one could stop them. They got experience, and they got good—especially when they stopped trying to make "conservative" product and instead focused on making a quality product with a secondary conservative message.

So, there was real talent there and . . . wait. Is that who I think it is? Wait, I gotta talk to him. Can we reschedule this?

15

VICTORY

"We Changed the Culture"

America is not perfect, but the conservative culture of the ascendant America of 2041 is far superior to the desperate, declining American culture under the progressive rule of Barack Obama and Hillary Clinton. Instead of a presumption that the government will meet its citizen's needs, the movement has shifted the society back to expecting every American to support himself. Some people choose poorly, but now consequences are seen not as something to be ameliorated through the resources of those who work but, instead, as something people who fail to meet their responsibilities must inevitably experience.

It is not necessarily an America that would thrill conservatives of 2009 in all respects. Monogamous gay couples are accepted as strengthening the family (the reemphasis on family, as opposed to enabling the extended post-college adolescence phenomenon of the early part of the century, is another huge achievement). Abortion is a peripheral issue, though it bubbles beneath the surface in a country where only a few states allow it and the culture frowns upon it. Marijuana is legal, but still scorned by most Americans.

There is also the challenge of governing for a generation that spent decades fighting and has little practical experience with the norms and customs of the democratic republic that it sought to restore. The "conservative court-packing" maneuver of President Marlowe still rankles many, including some conservatives who saw it as a victory of expedience over principle. That tension remains a challenge for an insurgency-turned-establishment. Someday, the government will no longer be conservative—that is inevitable. The question is whether the insurgency understands and will avoid making the same error the liberals made in running roughshod over the opposition.

But the progress under conservatism is undeniable even in the face of long-term challenges. The federal government is paying off the deficit, shrinking in size and scope, and returning its focus to appropriate areas like national defense. People speak and worship freely. The government no longer acts as the enforcer for big corporations with lobbyists and clout.

Perfect? No, but a hell of a lot better than it was under the progressives.

■ ■ ■

Ron Patel (President-Elect)

President Patel rubs his hands together to warm them before taking the final few steps up to the platform where the chief justice waits to administer the oath and where he will give his inaugural address.

I never doubted we'd win, not for a minute. I don't mean the election. I mean the whole struggle to take the country back from the progressives. We changed the culture.

It was long and hard, and sometimes it got really ugly, but I never doubted how it would end. We had an advantage they didn't. It was a huge advantage, huge. We were selling freedom. Yeah, we couldn't lose!

Tamara Hayes Smith (Professor/Activist)

The professor is working on a book of her own, a book that speculates about the cultural and political landscape in another 30 years. She shows me a synopsis, and to my surprise she predicts at least a brief flirtation with liberalism down the road within the next few election cycles.

While conservatives have succeeded for now, all political and cultural power is fleeting. We need to understand that. Even though we drove the culture right, it can still move left again if we let it.

There are no permanent victories. We defeated an ideology that placed elite-controlled collectivism above individuality, but the lure of the left will never die. Conservatives need to renew themselves again and again, because history has taught us that even the most dedicated conservative changes when he holds power for too long. He starts getting comfortable with it. And when that happens, it'll be time for a new insurgency.

Drew Johnson (TV Producer)

The soundstage seems almost empty, with technology having drastically reduced the size of production crews. However, there are more productions going on than ever, and they are spread all over the country—California is only slowly recovering from years of high taxes and high regulation that drove much of the media production out of the Golden State.

Drew and I stand off to the side, watching the cast rehearse for the new show that will tape (of course, it's all digital, but they still use the word "tape") later that evening.

If you can't laugh at yourself—the liberals never could—you are asking to be laughed at.

Television is now a generally conservative media, in the sense that the values it generally adopts tend to support family life, self-reliance, and liberty. That pretty much mirrors the culture at large—I'm still not clear whether we drove the culture back toward traditional values or whether the changed culture drove Hollywood back.

The whole nihilism thing with Hollywood was a dead end. You look at the television and movies of the 1960s through the 2010s, 50 years, and a lot of it was intensely cynical. It was supposed to be edgy not to believe in anything except the kind of vague liberal crap they spoon-fed us in schools and universities.

You would see that the conservatives were always the villains—always. Any kind of positive value was always faked, never sincere. If a religious person showed up, you just knew—there's the villain. He'd be a hypocrite or worse. I always hated that kind of cheap cynicism. They never had anything better to offer; it was always about cutting down regular people and their traditions and values.

Yeah, I was conservative, but I was an artist first. I still am. And what I saw with this liberal lockstep thinking was boring and stupid product. So I decided I would rise within the system, get my own show, and do what I wanted. And I found that showing up smug liberals and their nonsense got this huge response.

Pretty soon other people were doing it. Now, I wasn't the first. The real break came a few years before, when Obamacare totally tanked and a few—not all—of the late night comics turned on him. Until then he had been untouchable—no one would dare make a joke about him. But eventually there was enough of a payoff for being brave enough to take him on that at least a few couldn't resist.

The lapdog comics and hosts who stuck by him and sucked up to him, well, they all went away. It wasn't just that they were liberal. It was because you lose credibility when you try to be a man of the people and you can't talk about what the people are talking about.

There was some direct action too. Some conservatives began to actively boycott liberal entertainment. Some liberal would say something horrible about conservatives in general, or more often make some disgusting comment about a conservative woman, and Twitter and Facebook and other social media would ignite. The conservatives would simply stop watching. Now, a niche show on one of the old cable networks could survive that, but on the big networks it was a real problem. Liberals would retaliate and urge their folks to tune in to counterbalance it, but it's a lot easier to organize a view-out than a view-in, if you see what I mean.

So, it started becoming acceptable to joke about liberals, and joking about conservatives got to be kind of tired and hacky. Now, liberals are often the butt of jokes. They usually get portrayed as bitter, out of touch, and borderline delusional. Now, I'd argue that's all absolutely true. Liberals are all those things and worse. I happen to think liberals are inherently funnier because they're so obnoxious and their failures are so undeniable.

Are we doing to them what they did to us? I hope so. Look, I don't buy the idea of equivalency. Liberalism is a failure—we lived through decades of it. It is opposed to freedom—we all saw how the liberals ignored the Constitution to keep power, even if it meant sticking some critics in jail. Liberalism makes people stupid, lazy, and weak. I'm all for it being mocked because it's terrible.

But we conservatives have to make sure not to allow our new cultural power to turn us reactionary or allow us to fall prey to powerful interests. Power always corrupts, and I expect it will with us in the entertainment world—hell, I expect it will in the entire culture. This next generation is going to find fault with us, and that's okay. I just hope the people who take us out when we get fat, lazy, and corrupt are more conservative than we are!

Jack Archer (Democratic Strategist)

When the retired Democratic strategist talks about the past, you can read the disappointment on his face. It was clear that at one time he believed in liberalism. It is not so clear that his current support for it is based on anything more than habit.

270   You need to understand something about Obama. He always—always—succeeded because his opponents screwed up. He

waited for it. But the GOP made him be aggressive, and he just wasn't that good at it. I wish our party today would stop "me tooing" them and start fighting them like they fought us!

But I don't see that happening for a while. The Obamacare thing was really the first domino. It was so incompetently executed, and the fact was that if the Democrats had been upfront about how it was going to really turn everyone's healthcare insurance upside down, it never would have passed. And then they just wouldn't stop digging once they got into the hole. People would be upset and they would essentially tell them that they were too stupid to understand all the liberals were doing for them. Liberals had gotten away with a lot in the past, but you couldn't deny what people saw with their own eyes.

And then Hillary comes in and tries to salvage all these programs that, while well intentioned, were just falling apart and becoming unsustainable. Not just Obamacare—Medicaid, food stamps, everything. All the while the economy is still tanking for everyone except the politicians' rich friends on Wall Street. These were Democrats and they were cavorting with rich guys! How the hell was I supposed to spin that!

I was a strategist trying to find a way to win our campaigns. You know how hard it is to sell a product that stinks and that everyone knows stinks? In the 1950s it was the Ford Edsel. In the 1980s, New Coke. In the 2020s, the iPhone 19.

I don't think the damn conservatives killed liberalism. I think liberals did by not being honest, competent liberals.

Michael Ambarian (Supreme Court Justice)

The justice ponders the activist conservative Supreme Court of today as he orders another pint of Guinness.

271

Do I have doubts about using the courts to promote a constitutional conservative agenda? Hell no. Not a one. Constitutional conservatism is about conserving the Constitution, not about substituting in the latest leftist legal fad du jour. There's your difference.

We learned from Justice Roberts that when you play constitutional footsie with progressives, their foot kicks your ass. No, I have zero problem with activism in support of the Constitution. We ought to be *more* active in support of it."

Roberta Klein (Conservative Activist/Attorney)

The renowned lawyer sums up the fight that took three decades of her career.

We never gave an inch—we fought attacks on free speech, freedom of the press, free exercise of religion, the right to keep and bear arms, and the right to be free of unreasonable searches. The thing about progressives is that, unlike us, for them these freedoms were always merely tools to use to batter their opponents. They never really held them as principles and never had a moment's hesitation in abridging them once they had power.

But for constitutional conservatives, these were bedrock, core beliefs. And the American people saw who fought for them. In the minds of most Americans, constitutional conservatism became the ideology associated with freedom. And when you thought of progressivism, you thought of the smug bureaucrat who denied your request for a doctor's appointment.

Billy Coleman (Activist)

Billy has shopping to do—at a midsized grocery store whose owner
he has known since high school. He picks up his hemp shopping bag
and leaves me with a thought.

Might Walmart come back someday? Kind of up to it. If it
wants to play by the same rules as everyone else, it's welcome to
try. But the days when a corporation can use the government to
crush the little guy and erase the competition, well, those days
are over.

I gotta get my shopping done and get back to the farm—my
cows won't milk themselves.

Ted Jindal (Technology Consultant)

The master technologist activates the HP holograph monitor and
gestures toward it with evident pride, as well as evident concern.

This is our encrypted database. It has everyone we know or
believe is a constitutional conservative, and we interact with
them constantly. There's a phenomenon we call "tech exhaus-
tion" where a person gets tired of constant contact over social
media, but we see surprisingly little of it. Most conservatives
have learned you have to watch these bastards like hawks, and
we do that for them and pass them the info they need to stamp
out liberalism wherever is raises its pointy little head. They
learned the hard way—if you aren't engaged, the bad guys still
will be.

Brad Fields (Insurance Salesman)

Brad has to take a call from a client, but leaves me with some final thoughts.

I feel like today we have the country that the Founders promised us. Some people are angry because there's no more free lunch. I say, "Great!" Government is supposed to protect people and allow them to live their lives freely, not to subsidize deadbeats.

You know what I want from the federal government? A military that can kill our enemies, guards on our borders to make sure you can't come in without an invitation, and not a helluva lot else. If it isn't in the Constitution, the federal government has no business doing it. Period.

But most of all, it needs to leave me and my family alone.

Sammy Honda (Hollywood Producer)

The valet glides the Ford Ventura up to us as we wait on the curb. Honda is so busy talking to me that he doesn't notice, but then again it's electric so the producer probably didn't even hear it. A few decades ago, no one in Tinseltown would have been caught dead driving an American car, but Ford's refusal to be bailed out and the massive technological advances that came about after Marlowe's deregulation initiatives during the 2020s and 2030s put the venerable automaker back on top as the car the Tinseltown players drive—or, rather, ride in while the auto-drive sweeps them to their destinations.

The valet waits with the door open as Honda finishes telling me about his next project.

I'm making a movie about the Iranian War. Lots of action, but with a message, you know? That message is, don't be a punk if you're president!

It's going to really drill the libs. It's written by this Gallegos guy who fought in it. It's harsh. It shows how Clinton and her gang talked big, got our boys to hang their asses out over the line, then left them hanging. It never could have been made before.

Flamenco (Performance Artist)

With a performance happening in a half hour, the artist talks to me while changing into an outfit consisting of a pink skullcap, a leather jacket, and what the artist describes as an "enqueered Lebanese kilt."

Flamenco cares nothing for politics now. Flamenco does not need to. Flamenco pays some of Flamenco's income in taxes, Flamenco is left alone. This is the way it should be.

Government should be off in the background, out of our lives—though Flamenco always votes, and for the most conservative candidate. Without interference by bossy liberals, Flamenco can concentrate on new projects. Currently, Flamenco is examining identity issues by rejecting the use of the first person in everyday speech.

Gail Partridge (Leftist Show Host)

Partridge fulminates, enraged that the progressive world of 2009 has morphed into her own version of hell in 2041.

This isn't my country anymore. People like me get no say at all. People are doing whatever they want, with no guidance, no leadership, totally out of control. You call that freedom?

True freedom is freedom from having to do everything for yourself. I think people will miss when we had a government that took the load off their shoulders, a government that let people with some education make decisions instead of just anyone.

Supposedly everyone is making money today, but why are we only discussing material issues? What about morality? When Obama was president, yes, we had a few problems, but we were a moral country. Now, someone like me who wants to put progress in motion gets laughed at. It shameful.

I love what this country was 30 years ago, but I hate it today. America doesn't deserve liberalism!

EPILOGUE

The following is newly sworn-in President Robert Manuel Patel's inauguration speech, given on January 20, 2041, in its entirety:

My fellow Americans, we gather here today to continue our work to fulfill the vision of the Founding Fathers. As such, upon today taking office as president of the United States, I shall be brief, for the responsibilities of the federal government as set forth in our Constitution are few.

We have come far as a nation, yet we have truly come full circle. After over a century of misguided expansion of the role of the federal government, thinking this would make us more prosperous and free, we instead found ourselves much less prosperous and much less free. Today, embracing the principles of the Founders, our nation once again stands above all other nations in terms of material wealth and military power, but most importantly, in terms of freedom.

For without freedom, wealth simply means life inside a gilded cage. That is not a fit life for any American.

The Constitution clearly sets forth my duties and the limits upon my authority. I shall endeavor to perform those duties to the best of my ability, and no others. Under our system of limited government, a president who does more than the enumerated duties our Constitution sets forth is as great a failure as one who fails to carry out his enumerated duties.

I shall lead the executive branch and see that it faithfully carries out its duties under the Constitution and the laws promulgated under its authority—all of the laws, not merely those I pick and choose according to my whims and my own short-term political interests.

I shall endeavor to make the executive branch ever smaller but ever more efficient, and to ensure that its employees understand that their ultimate accountability is to the citizens.

I shall lead the military as the commander in chief, a great and grave responsibility. Our military has once again assumed its rightful place as the most powerful in the world, but its true distinction remains that the United States military is the greatest agent of peace, freedom, and justice in all of human history.

The protection of our nation is properly the president's most important duty, and the fighting men and women who stand between us and our enemies—for we must never again delude ourselves into believing that we have no enemies—will always be foremost in my mind.

But what I shall not do as president is presume to lead you. Nowhere in the Constitution is the president denominated the "leader" of the nation; he or she is only an executive with carefully defined responsibilities for certain specified and limited parts of federal government. I am not, and do not propose to be, your guide, your teacher, or your master. The president is not a ruler; he is a servant, an employee hired by you, our citizens, to perform certain tasks. He is nothing more.

As a nation, we once forgot that. We chose to look not to ourselves but to a remote potentate cloistered in his imperial chambers in the capital to provide the guidance we should have sought within ourselves or from our Creator.

And some presidents, human beings with human weaknesses, came to believe that they had not merely the ability but the right to rule their fellow citizens.

No president rules any American. An American citizen is free, with rights granted by his Creator. Through the Constitution, the citizens grant the government certain powers, but no more than are clearly enumerated.

You, the American citizen, by right, rules the president. Now, once again you do, and for as long as I am your president, you will.

May God bless you, and may God bless the United States of America.

AFTERWORD

"I have not yet begun to fight!"

—Captain John Paul Jones, United States Navy

We built this country. We fought for it. It's ours, and we're taking it back.

The fight to take back America from the progressives will not be just a battle, or even a campaign. It will be a figurative war, and a long one. We need to understand that returning America to what it should be will take a generation, maybe two, and especially in the early years we will face defeat after defeat.

And there will be thuggery—threats, intimidation, even minor violence—committed by our enemies against us, designed to silence us. We are seeing that already. They ignore laws, rules, and traditions when it suits them—even when they can be seen on video vehemently arguing the now inconvenient contrary position.

They lie to our faces and tell us we're stupid for having believed them. They convert the word "period" from meaning "no exceptions" into an all-purpose asterisk that converts whatever they say into whatever they happen to need it to mean at any given moment.

We need to be tough enough to accept all this, to face the challenge as it is and not as we wish it to be. If we are, we will grow strong enough to prevail in this struggle.

Today, we constitutional conservatives are the minority faction of a minority party—many of our opponents are those supposedly on our side, who call themselves "conservatives" back home at election time, then come to Washington and gleefully vote to sustain and expand the hideous, soul-killing welfare state and its attendant pathologies.

These pseudocons—call them "moderates," "squishes," "RINOs," or "McCains"—hate us even more than they hate the liberals. We seek their removal; the liberals are content to let them enjoy a few perks as the loyal opposition, so long as they manifest that loyalty by not actually opposing anything. So we, not the real enemy, are their target.

Our opponents, therefore, have us surrounded. This is good. It means we can attack in any direction.

So, how does one fight outnumbered and outgunned? How can anyone in our position ever hope to win? I bet General George Washington wondered that as his forces lost battle after battle against the most powerful military in the world right up until the time the British cried "uncle" and the rebels won it all.

You win because you believe in your cause. We fight for principles. We believe in America and the promise of freedom and liberty embodied in the Constitution. Our main opponents—the welfare state liberals and the submissive Tories of the Republican establishment—believe only in retaining the perks and privileges of power.

They don't stand a chance.

Our strategy—the blend of the means (resources) at our disposal with the available ways (the possible courses of action we can undertake) to reach the end we seek (a Constitution-based, free nation where individuals govern their own lives while also taking responsibility for them)—presents us only one real option. We must undertake a multifront, long-term political, social, and cultural insurgency designed to seize society's high ground in order to restore the Founders' vision. It's not a struggle of violence but one of persuasion and action. Our weapons are not arms but arguments.

How does a force that is always "losing" end up winning? That's the key question.

We need to fight smarter. We need to maximize our many strengths—and we have incredible strengths, starting with our message—while minimizing our weaknesses. We need to learn to hit our opponents not where they are strong, but where they are weak. We need to be agile, and to avoid allowing them to put their full strength against us.

We will pick at them until, exhausted and defeated, they collapse as we flow in to fill the vacuum. The looming final failure of Obamacare is only the beginning.

We need to prioritize our efforts, as any good insurgency does. And we need to accept that we don't get a vote on reality. We need to approach reality in a way that supports our constitutional conservative objectives. We won't achieve every policy objective—after all, we do not seek to be dictators. We must

283

not become fixed on single issues while pursuing a wider vision. The alternative may be to lose the entire war instead of just a skirmish.

Remember that picking a hill to die on results in you dying. We're not interested in our cause dying on principle. Conservatism is too important to let that happen. Let progressivism do the dying.

This is not about losing gloriously but about winning gloriously.

The current cliché is that the Tea Party is dead. Nonsense. We're still here. We're still ready to fight. And we're going to fight.

We're going to do so each in our own way, whether by infiltrating liberal institutions or using social media to participate in campaigns or simply modeling the benefits of a conservative lifestyle to regular Americans who have been brainwashed into thinking that government-subsidized degeneracy is their only option.

Remember that we are fighting a bloated, slow opponent. It hits hard only because it is so massive, wielding government force and media power, but it has to find you and hold you still to hit you. We have to be gone when they land a blow. We need to select our targets carefully, put our own power against their vulnerabilities, and leave the other side damaged, disorganized, and demoralized.

We need to drive our enemies to fits trying to find us, forcing them to play Conservative Whac-a-Mole as they get more and more exhausted trying to club us.

And we need allies. Libertarians first of all—we agree on much more than we disagree on, though our disagreements are real. But how about some people who think they are "liberal" but aren't? These are people who value family, country, and hard work but for whatever reason—including the fog of propaganda disgorged by our opponents—they think *we* are the enemy.

And what about young people? We offer the opportunity to be more than a nation of hapless, eternally adolescent Julias. We also offer the chance to rebel against the stifling nannyism that has tormented young people from the day they set foot in the unionized conformity factories known as "public schools" to the petty fascist tyranny of the leftist-controlled universities. We need to seize the mantle of the rebel, the nonconformist, the individual.

We are cool, not these tatted-up, goateed conformists who share every stupid idea, notion, and prejudice with the rest of their boring, pseudointellectual clique. Wanna fight the power? Welcome to our struggle.

If this book did its job, it will leave you with both hope and inspiration. No insurgency can succeed if its participants do not believe that it will eventually prevail. That's why the mainstream media is so intent on telling you how America has embraced liberalism and that you are alone, a freak, and a rejected relic of America's wicked racist, sexist, imperialist, and homophobic past.

It's all a lie—just look at how desperate they are to convince you.

The liberals protest too much. They know the enforced mediocrity, conformity, and squalor of their twisted ideology is poison to real Americans. They know that what we sell sells itself to those with self-respect and pride. This is why they are so busy undercutting those qualities with their government handouts.

We cannot lose—you should not merely have hope but the serene assurance that it is only a matter of time before America is once again that shining city on the hill and no longer a squalid slum in the swamp.

And, hopefully, you will be inspired to join the fight. How will you contribute? I don't know. *You* know your capabilities, your resources, and your priorities better than anyone. *You* decide how you can best contribute.

You don't need me to tell you what to do. You're an American. You're an adult. Think about how best you can help, and you'll know what to do.

Then go do it.

And someday—yes, years from now—we will look around us at a restored America, and feel the pride of knowing that when our country's most sacred values and principles were under merciless attack, we fought to take America back.

Kurt Schlichter
May 2014

ABOUT THE AUTHOR

KURT SCHLICHTER is a weekly columnist for *Townhall.com*. His freelance work has been published in the *New York Post*, the *Washington Examiner*, the *Los Angeles Times*, the *Boston Globe*, the *Washington Times*, *Army Times*, the *San Francisco Examiner*, and elsewhere.

A stand-up comic for several years, Kurt was personally recruited by Andrew Breitbart, and since 2009 his writings on political and cultural issues have been regularly published in the "Big Hollywood," "Big Government," "Big Journalism," and "Big Peace" sections of the Breitbart.com website.

Kurt is an active Twitter (@KurtSchlichter) user whose biting Twitter commentary led to him writing *I Am a Conservative: Uncensored, Undiluted, and Absolutely Un-PC*, *I Am a Liberal: A Conservative's Guide to Dealing with Nature's Most Irritating Mistake*, and *Fetch My Latte: Sharing Feelings with Stupid People*. All three e-books reached number one on the Amazon Kindle "Political Humor" bestseller list.

Kurt has served as a news source, an on-screen commentator, and a guest on nationally syndicated radio programs regarding political, military, and legal issues, including *Fox News, The*

Hugh Hewitt Show, *The Larry Elder Show*, *The Dennis Miller Show*, *Geraldo*, *The John Phillips Show*, *The Tony Katz Show*, PJTV's *The Conversation*, *The Tamara Jackson Show*, *The Delivery with Jimmie Bise, Jr.*, *The Dana Loesch Show*, *The Point*, the *WMAL Washington Morning Show with Larry O'Connor*, *The Derek Hunter Show*, and *The Snark Factor*, among others. Kurt appears weekly on the *Cam and Company* show, and averages four to five other media appearances a week.

Kurt is a successful trial lawyer and name partner in a Los Angeles law firm representing Fortune 500 companies and individuals in matters ranging from routine business cases to confidential Hollywood disputes. A member of the Million Dollar Advocates Forum, which recognizes attorneys who have won trial verdicts in excess of $1 million, his litigation strategy and legal analysis articles are regularly published in legal publications such as the *Los Angeles Daily Journal* and *California Lawyer*.

Kurt is a 1994 graduate of Loyola Law School, where he was a law review editor. He majored in communications and political science as an undergraduate at the University of California, San Diego, where he edited the conservative student paper *California Review* while also writing a regular column in the student humor paper *The Koala*.

Kurt served as a US Army infantry officer on active duty and in the California Army National Guard, reaching the rank of full colonel. He wears the silver "jump wings" of a paratrooper and commanded the elite 1st Squadron, 18th Cavalry Regiment. A veteran of both the Persian Gulf War and Operation Enduring Freedom (Kosovo), he is a graduate of the Army's Combined Arms and Services Staff School, the Command and General Staff College, and the United States Army War College, where he received a master of strategic studies degree.